15 MINUTE STORAGE MEALS

QUICK HEALTHFUL RECIPES
& FOOD STORAGE HANDBOOK

by
Jayne Benkendorf

Published by
Ludwig Publishing
Edmond, OK

15 MINUTE STORAGE MEALS:
Quick, Healthful Recipes & Food Storage Handbook
by Jayne Benkendorf
Incudes index. ISBN: 0-9651990-2-9

15 MINUTE STORAGE MEALS:
Quick, Healthful Recipes & Food Storage Handbook
by Jayne Benkendorf
Copyright 1999 by Jayne Benkendorf

Printed in the United States of America by:
RG Printing
706 W. California
Oklahoma City, OK 73102

Book cover design by: Tim Duncan, RG Printing, Oklahoma City, OK

DISCLAIMER:
It should be noted that in no way is any information contained herein to be construed as a prescription or medical advice, or is this information in any way to preclude the need or advice of a health professional. In fact, it is recommended that should you wish to change your diet because of any information contained herein, you should first consult a health professional, especially if you are currently taking medication and/or have a physical impairment. All rights reserved. If you do not wish to be bound by the above, you may return this book for a full refund to:

Meals In Minutes
P.O. Box 1828
Edmond, OK 73083-1828

TABLE OF CONTENTS

In all affairs it's a healthy thing now and then to hang a question mark on the things you have long taken for granted.

- Bertrand Russell

THE "FABULOUS 30", HIGH ENERGY FOODS
WHAT ARE THE "FABULOUS 30" FOODS?

The "Fabulous 30" foods are the best of the best. These are the foods that I use as the main ingredients in all of my meals. These are all very high energy foods. They're very rich in complex carbohydrates. These foods will not, and I stress will NOT, convert to fat easily. Research clearly indicates that any society, any group of people, or any person who dominates their diet with these type foods will NOT have weight problems. These foods are energy foods. They convert to energy easily - not to fat easily. These foods are to our bodies what high octane fuel is to our car. These are our high octane foods.

While most meals are planned around some kind of meat, the "Fabulous 30" concept is to plan meals around these high octane foods. When meats and dairy products dominate our diet, two problems occur. First these foods are not effective energy foods. For example, athletes have learned that these are the type foods that must be limited or eliminated prior to competition. Secondly, meats and dairy products can be high in fat, and foods high in fat convert to fat very easily. Please understand, I am not saying we should never eat meat and dairy products. Quite the contrary, as they supply valuable nutrients. All I'm saying is that they should not dominate our meals. In fact, I think our total intake of these type foods should be kept to 10% or less of our total food consumption.

Another common error we make in meal planning is with the use of highly processed foods, primarily the grains and the sugars. These type foods certainly dominate many of our meals. These foods are everywhere in our grocery stores, but we must not let these type foods dominate our meals. Why?

Highly processed foods have had most of their nutrients and fiber removed during processing. These foods leave our body still hungry. Have you ever eaten and eaten until you're stuffed, but you're still hungry? With these highly processed foods, we overeat because we are not giving our body what it needs. In addition, highly processed foods convert to fat more easily than their whole counterparts. For example, whole wheat bread is a very high energy food, whereas the highly processed white bread, in my opinion, does nothing more than add inches to the hips!

There are no highly processed foods in the "Fabulous 30" foods. In fact, the "Fabulous 30" are clearly at the other end of the scale - very high in nutrients, very high in fiber and very high in energy. With these foods you will find, as I have, that you will get full before you get stuffed!

WHAT ABOUT THE "FABULOUS 30" RECIPES?

I have created complete meals which are dominated by one or more of the "Fabulous 30" foods. These are truly very high energy meals. These meals are put together using the basic concept that 50% to 60% of any meal should come from the high octane, energy foods; 30% to 40% should come from fresh or frozen fruits and vegetables; and not more that 10% from animal products, fats, and highly processed foods.

I assure you, that if we adopt a lifestyle of eating whole foods in the proportions that are illustrated in these recipes, we will see our energy level increase, our attitude become more positive, and our weight problem begin to disappear.

These are the 30 recipes that I use the most. They are time tested. They work!

This is the incredible part. These meals take 15 minutes to get to the table!! I certainly don't like spending a lot of time in the kitchen, nor do I like washing a bunch of dirty pots and pans! I want good quality meals, but I don't want to take a lot of time fixing them. If you're like I am, you'll love these recipes!

WHY DIETS DON'T WORK

We starve ourselves, we limit calories, we count fat grams, we weigh our food, we measure our food, we use sugar substitutes, we use fat substitutes, we skip meals, we eat all sorts of crazy food combinations, and we keep on gaining weight - and we keep on going on diets. It's obvious, DIETS DON'T WORK!

I want to share this incident with you. A few years back a woman came to me in tears. She was literally crying. She said, "Jayne, I'm a failure. I don't know what I'm doing wrong." She told me, "10 years ago I was a little overweight, about 10 pounds. I went on a diet, and I lost the 10 pounds, but I gained it back plus some more. For 10 years I have done everything. I have been on every program around. I've tried them all." She was actually boo-hooing at this point. And she said, "Just look at me. I'm 60 pounds overweight! I don't have any energy, I hate myself, I'm depressed, I'm no fun to be around. What am I doing wrong?"

I got her calmed down, then I asked her one question. "Mary, during these last 10 years, have you gone hungry a lot?" I thought she was going to attack me. She jumped up, and said, "Are you crazy!

I'm hungry all the time! Don't you know anything about diets? You have to go hungry to lose weight." This lady was beside herself.

Well, I calmed her down again and told her about how I spent 20 years on those stupid diets and if she thinks she did some silly things listen to some of mine. Do you know about the grapefruit diet that is supposed to 'melt away' the fat? Or how about this one; for 2 weeks I ate nothing but bananas and buttermilk! How stupid can you get! After 20 years of this I finally woke up and said to myself, "Hey, Jayne, something's wrong." So I began doing some soul searching and a lot of studying, and it all of a sudden dawned on me what I had been doing wrong and it's so simple! I was starving myself into overweightness! And from then on I came to realize that if I were to get control of my body and achieve permanent weight control, I had to follow this key rule: Never Go Hungry! Etch that in your brain: NEVER GO HUNGRY!

Why is this so important? Well, let's just see what happens to our bodies when we go hungry. First of all, when we don't eat, we're telling our bodies to conserve energy. Our bodies have a natural built-in survival instinct. Let's say we got caught out in the desert with only one canteen of water. Would we drink it all at once, or would we ration it and make it last? Of course, we would make it last. This is exactly what our bodies do naturally when we restrict food. It holds onto our calories and rations them.

If we get in a pattern of not eating meals, or we restrict calories, our brain sends a message to the body to conserve energy. Now what does this mean? It means we don't burn calories. We hang onto them. Oh boy, do we hang on! When this happens, our metabolism slows down and our energy decreases. Then, now get this, when we do eat a meal, our bodies won't burn these calories, at least not very well, because the body remembers that it's not going to get anymore for quite a few hours, and the calories are stored as fat. That ugly stuff - fat. In a nutshell, this is why diets that restrict calories don't work. They never have and they never will!

Now, I'm not saying we won't lose weight if we restrict enough calories. We will. But the problem occurs when we start eating again - and we always do! We have trained our bodies to conserve energy, to hang onto our calories and to store these calories as fat. In other words, when we go on a diet, we're actually training ourselves to accumulate fat.

Studies are clearly telling us that when we eat the right foods, we can eat all we want, and we will not gain weight. As a well known promoter of the "Never Go Hungry" theory says, "Food does not make you fat. Fat makes you fat." This is so true. Think of this:

7

Why will a person gain weight when he or she eats 2,000 calories of the typical American diet (which is close to 40% fat); yet will lose weight when they eat 2,000 calories of predominately high energy food? The answer is simple: Energy foods do not convert to fat easily. They convert to energy. They keep our metabolism moving in high gear. They give us the energy to exercise. They're what give us pep; the get-up-and-go.

Do you know what the difference is between a couch potato with a negative attitude and an active, energetic person with a positive attitude? About 30 to 60 days of practicing the "Never Go Hungry" concepts and dominating the diet with the "Fabulous 30" foods.

If you're struggling with weight problems, I know what you're going through. I've been there. I also know the freedom we can enjoy without having this terrible yoke around our neck!

A WORD ABOUT EXERCISE

Regular exercise should become a natural part of our lives. However, when we do not eat energy foods, we simply do not have the energy to exert energy. We feel sluggish and develop the attitude of not really caring. This will change as you begin dominating your meals with the energy foods.

As your energy increases you need to add some form of exercise to your lifestyle. You may start by simply walking up a flight of stairs instead of using the elevator. Activity will actually begin to grow on you!

Two things happen to us when we exercise regularly. First, we keep our body's metabolism running in high gear. This is necessary for good health. It keeps our mind active, our organs functioning well, and it burns calories. Secondly, exercise builds muscle, and muscle tone makes our body look and move better. Years of dieting takes its toll on our muscles. Restricting calories causes our body to live off its own muscles, and the only way we can replace these muscles is through exercise.

I am often asked what kind of exercise is best. My only answer is this: The kind we enjoy the most. Generally, anything is better than what we have been doing. Personally, I enjoy dance aerobics; however, some people enjoy walking, jogging, stationary biking, Jazzercise, etc. You can join a club or you can participate at home.

In the future we'll be seeing more and more companies allowing time for their employees to exercise while at work. Evidence is very clear that periods of exercise during the day increase our productivity. However, the important thing for us is this: As our energy level increases because of our improved eating habits, it will be easier for us to exercise - and we will want to!

GROUPING FOODS FOR WEIGHT CONTROL

If we eat the right assortment of healthful foods, we should never have to go hungry, never have to count calories, and we won't be afraid of those bathroom scales! When we group foods for weight control - and good health, we must ask two basic questions: Does this food convert to energy easily? Or, does this food convert to fat easily? By answering these two questions about all our foods, we can see that they fall into three basic food groups.

GROUP I (Fiber Rich, Energy Efficient Foods)

Foods in this group include all whole grains and whole grain products, all legumes and all complex carbohydrate vegetables. Foods in this group are good sources of fiber and are our very best energy foods. In other words, when we eat these foods, our bodies convert them to energy easily. In addition, and of great importance to us, these foods do not convert to fat easily.

These type foods should dominate our meals - 50% to 60% of our food intake should come from these foods. Athletes and individuals in special training programs will "jump" their intake of the energy foods up to 70% to 80%. The bottom line for us is this: Energy foods must dominate our food intake for optimum weight control and wellness.

This is what the "Fabulous 30" foods are all about. The "Fabulous 30" identifies our very best energy foods - the foods I personally eat for energy. Plan your meals around these foods, and you too will have permanent weight control, increased energy and a strong positive attitude - one that says, "Look out world, here I come!"

GROUP II (Fiber Rich, Neutral Energy Foods)

Foods in this group are the fruits and vegetables. They are just like the foods in Group I in that they are fiber rich and will not convert to fat easily. The difference is that these foods are not as high in energy.

From a health standpoint, we derive a tremendous amount of our nutrients from these foods, and they must be included in our diets. Without these foods, we would not realize all the benefits from the energy foods. We can fill our car with the very best high energy fuel available, but if our spark plugs aren't working right, we're wasting our money. Likewise, we can eat all the right energy foods, but if we do not include a generous supply of fruits and vegetables along with them, they won't be energized.

Remember, 50% to 60% of our food intake should come from the energy foods. Likewise, 30% to 40% of our food intake should come from fruits and vegetables. And how should our fruits and vegetables be eaten?

The very best is raw or lightly cooked or steamed. I do not think any canned fruit and most canned vegetables are good choices. (Canned tomatoes, legumes and some soups are exceptions.) I prefer fresh or frozen fruits and vegetables because they contain the most natural nutrients. Fruits and vegetables are fragile, and nutrients can be destroyed very easily. Overcooking is definitely not recommended.

GROUP III (Fiberless, Inefficient Energy Foods)

Foods in this group include all meats, dairy products, fats (butter, margarine, cooking oils, mayonnaise, salad dressings, etc.) and all highly processed foods.

These foods contain very little or no fiber and do not convert to energy efficiently. The body just loves to store these type foods as fat! They convert very easily to fat in and on our bodies. It's little wonder we have so many weight problems in the United States because these foods dominate our diet. The key here is dominate. We need not eliminate these foods as some of them supply nutrients we need.

Lean meats and nonfat dairy products are our best choices, but they still should not amount to more than 10% of our total food intake. Most people find it difficult to reduce these foods to 10%, but this is because they're not replacing these foods with energy foods.

The whole concept of the "Never Go Hungry" eating lifestyle is just that: When we're hungry–eat! Just make sure it comes from foods in Groups I and II, not from foods in Group III.

A PARTIAL LISTING OF FOODS
WITHIN EACH FOOD GROUP:

GROUP I

WHOLE GRAINS
  Bagels
  Biscuits*
  Bread
  Cereal
  Corn
  Crackers*
  Grits
  Pancakes*
  Pasta
  Popcorn, raw
Rice
  Tortillas, plain
  Waffles*
  Wheat Germ

LEGUMES
  Black Beans
  Blackeye Peas
  Garbanzos
  Green Peas
  Kidney Beans
  Lentils
  Lima Beans
  Navy Beans
  Pinto Beans
  Red Beans
  Potatoes
  Sweet Potatoes
  White Potatoes

WINTER SQUASH
  Acorn
  Butternut
  Hubbard
  Spaghetti

Made with minimal fat

GROUP II

VEGETABLES
  Asparagus
  Beets
  Broccoli
  Carrots
  Celery
  Cucumber
  Garlic
  Kale
  Leaf Lettuce
  Mushrooms
  Mustard Greens
  Okra
  Onions
  Parsley
  Sweet Peppers
  Spinach
  Summer Squash
    Crookneck
    Scallop
    Zucchini
  Tomatoes
  Turnips

FRUITS
  Apples
  Apricots
  Bananas
  Berries (all)
  Cantaloupe
  Grapefruit
  Grapes
  • Nectarines
  Melons (all)
  Oranges
  Peaches
  Pears
  Pineapple
  Plums

GROUP III

MEATS
  Beef
  Chicken
  Fish
  Pork
  Turkey

DAIRY PRODUCTS
  Buttermilk
  Cheese
  Cottage Cheese
  Cream Cheese
  Frozen Yogurt
  Ice Cream
  Milk
  Sour Cream
  Yogurt

FATS
  Butter
  Cooking Oil
  Margarine
  Mayonnaise
  Salad Dressing

NUTS & SEEDS
  (Roasted in Oil)

EGGS

HIGHLY PROCESSED
FOODS
  Candies
  Jellies
  Junk Foods
  Pastries
  White Breads
  White Flour

PLEASE NOTE:

You will notice that raw nuts and seeds are not included in any of these three food groups. They are an exception as they are an energy and a high fat food combined. My favorites are almonds, pecans and sunflower seeds. I use these often for flavor and crunch in many foods. They are very nutritious and give us energy, but since they are high in fat, they should be somewhat limited. Just remember, only the raw choices are acceptable.

SUMMARY:

You're holding in your hands, right now, the answer to the question, "What should I eat - to lose weight, stay trim and be healthy?" *15 Minute Storage Meals: Quick, Healthful Recipes & Food Storage Handbook* that utilizes the "Fabulous 30" foods! These are the foods that dominate my meals and my snacks. I eat these foods when I'm hungry whether it's morning, noon or night - or somewhere in between. These foods do not make me fat. They will not make you fat. Only foods in Group III make us fat!

THE "FABULOUS 30" FOODS

CEREAL 1

My Choice: Kellogg's Nutri-Grain

There are quite a few cold cereals that I recommend as good energy food, and Kellogg's Nutri-Grain is one of my top choices. There are two varieties of Nutri-Grain. One is Almond Raisin which is a wheat free cereal made with whole grain brown rice, whole grain corn, raisins and almonds. The other variety is Nutri-Grain Golden Wheat made of whole grain wheat and whole grain corn.

These cereals are excellent energy foods and make a great quick-to-fix breakfast. Never, and I mean never, add sugar to such a good food. I don't feel a sweetener is needed; however, if you disagree, simply add a little concentrated apple juice and this should do the trick. Adding fresh or frozen fruit such as strawberries, peaches, or a banana will add to the taste and nutrition.

Most cereals on our shelves are nothing more than fat or sugar factories, so we must be selective. Some other cereals that are good choices include: Grape Nuts, Kellogg's All Bran, Weetabix, and Raisin Bran by Post, Skinners & Kellogg's. There are many good cereals, these are just a few of them.

FOR SWEETENING: Instead of sugar or sugar substitutes, use apple juice concentrate. All brands of frozen apple juice concentrate are fine. If you can get juice from organically grown apples, that's the best. Concentrated apple juice is very sweet and is an excellent substitute for sugar, not only on cereal but most any-place where we would use sweetening. We get the sweetness of the juice as well as the nutrients it provides. Sugar gives us no nutrients.

I keep a pitcher of thawed apple juice concentrate in the refrigerator all the time. Give it a try. I think you'll like it.

2 PASTA
My Choice: Hodgson Mill

Pasta is a tremendous energy food but, just like other grain products, only if it is of the whole grain variety. I know we have become accustomed to associating pasta with weight gain, but this is because of the rich sauces that are added and because of the type pasta that is eaten.

White pasta is much like white bread; it will convert to fat easier than the whole grain variety, and it does not supply as much energy. Traditional white pasta is made from semolina flour. Semolina is durum wheat that has been stripped of its germ and bran. (There go the vitamins, minerals, fiber and energy!)

Whole grain pasta is altogether a different story. Energy, fiber and nutrients make the difference. The best pasta is made from whole durum wheat, a hard wheat that is grown primarily in the northern, central states. It is this whole wheat that gives good pasta its unique taste and texture.

Whole wheat pasta has a rich, nutty flavor and is much more filling and satisfying - because it has all of its nutrients and fiber. I prefer the Hodgson Mill brand of pasta. The shape of pasta makes no difference; however I generally prefer the macaroni (elbow) shape because it is so easy for children to eat. But I use them all from time to time.

WHAT TO PUT ON PASTA: How about a pasta sauce? One of my favorite brands is Healthy Choice. Healthy Choice is very low in fat, and all varieties have a wonderful flavor and consistency. They're thick, not runny!

Some other brands are very high in fat, and some contain cottonseed oil - an ingredient I believe we should avoid. You see, cotton is not a food crop, therefore the pesticides are not regulated for food.

If you want to add cooked meat to your sauce, that's fine. Just be sure that it is very lean, and use only a small amount. My favorites to add to pasta sauce are chopped clams and chopped oysters.

BROWN RICE 3

My Choice:
There are many good brands of brown rice. I use Arrowhead Mills, Comet, Lundberg, Mahatma, S&W and Uncle Ben's.

Notice, we're talking about *brown* rice - not the white rice that dominates our grocery shelves and is served in so many restaurants. White rice is not completely bad and does supply energy, but not as much as the more natural brown rice. I always recommend and use brown rice.

What about quick cooking brown rice?

My Choice: Uncle Ben's, Minute, Arrowhead Mills, Success, and Gourmet Award

I was so excited when I first knew that quick cooking brown rice was available. It has been on the market for a few years, and quite a few manufacturers are carrying it.

Arrowhead Mills developed the technique that makes brown rice into a quick cooking rice. Regular brown rice is subjected to dry heat for a short period of time. The moisture that is inside each kernel turns to steam. When this steam is drawn out by the dry heat, it leaves tunnels inside the kernel. By this process, more surface area is created which enables the rice to be cooked in a shorter period of time.

Quick cooking brown rice contains the majority of the nutrients of the original brown rice, which makes it an excellent high energy, lowfat choice.

In my opinion, quick cooking brown rice does not have the flavor or texture of the long cooking rice, but I always keep it on hand for those times when I need rice really fast.

FOR FLAVORFUL RICE: Rice cooked in water doesn't have a lot of flavor. When I want more flavor, I cook rice in broth instead of water. If I want a poultry flavor, I use Swanson 1/3 Less Sodium Chicken Broth. When I want a beef flavor, I use Health Valley Beef Broth.

Many broths, and bouillons as well, contain MSG. These two products don't. (Swanson's regular chicken broth contains MSG, but not the 1/3 Less Sodium.)

2 WHOLE WHEAT BREAD

My Choice: 100% Whole Wheat by Earth Grains, Arnold, and Brownberry

When we're talking nutrition and energy, whole wheat bread has to be listed right at the top! Unfortunately, the real thing is sometimes hard to identify in the grocery store. Many, and I mean "a bunch", of the dark colored breads offered are only imposters with coloring added to make them look like whole wheat. These kinds are nothing more than white breads, and the only purpose I've figured out for them is putting extra pounds on my hips!

My favorite whole wheat bread choices are 100% Whole Wheat by Earth Grains, Arnold, and Brownberry.

WHAT TO PUT ON BREAD: If you're accustomed to putting a lot of butter on your bread, gradually decrease the amount you use until you no longer want butter. (This won't happen overnight, but it will happen.) Instead of butter, use a fruit jam made only with fruit and fruit juice. There are many good brands on the market. They include: Smucker's Simply Fruit, Polaner, R.W. Knudsen, Sorrell Ridge, and Poiret.

Also, try some apple butter on whole wheat toast. The brands I use are Smucker's Simply Fruit Apple Butter, L&A, and R.W. Knudsen.

BEANS (Legumes) 5

My Choice: Kidney Beans by S&W, Black Beans by Ranch Style, and Chili Hot Beans by Bush's

I eat a lot of beans. The beans I'm talking about are legumes; pintos, blackeye peas, garbanzos, kidneys, lentils, limas, etc. These beans are very low in fat (it's practically nonexistent) and are very high in energy.

I guess what I like most about beans, beside their taste, is that they can be used in so many different ways; in chili, in vegetable salads, pasta salads, in soups & stews, on potatoes–to name a few.

I will cook a pot of beans from "scratch", but I always keep canned beans in my pantry because they are so handy. I have three favorite kinds of canned beans; Chili Hot Beans by Bush's, Kidney Beans by S&W, and Black Beans by Ranch Style.

A bit about each of these wonderful legumes:
KIDNEY BEANS (S&W)

There are many brands of kidney beans on the market, but very few are free of ethylenediamine tetra-acetic acid (EDTA). EDTA is used to attract metal.

EDTA in food products attracts metals that are vital to good health: calcium, iron, zinc, magnesium, copper and others. Because of this mineral loss, many health professionals recommend that pregnant and nursing women avoid foods with EDTA. I'm certainly not pregnant or nursing, but I don't want robbed of calcium, or any of the other valuable nutrients.

One of my favorite brands of kidney beans is S&W. S&W also has a 50% Less Salt variety. This is much lower in sodium than the regular variety, but it still is a bit high in sodium. With either variety, if you need to watch your sodium intake, rinse the beans well with running water.

21

BLACK BEANS (Ranch Style)

Black Beans by Ranch Style is one of my favorite brands. Did you know that black beans are great added to a vegetable salad? Since they're high in sodium, you may want to rinse them with running water, then add them to your greens and chopped vegetables.

Use them in all sorts of Mexican dishes. A fun lunch I like to make is a burrito sort of thing. Just do this:

To a corn tortilla, add some fresh spinach leaves; top with a couple tablespoons of rinsed black beans, top those with chopped tomatoes and green onions. If you'd like, sprinkle a little shredded low moisture, part skim mozzarella cheese on the very top. Now, microwave for about 30 seconds or so.

If you'd like some extra zip, add some salsa. (I like Pace Picante Sauce.) This is so quick to fix, is very attractive and very tasty.

Beans are relatively inexpensive, but if food were priced based on the energy it supplied, beans would be that higher priced, super unleaded fuel!

CHILI HOT BEANS (BUSH'S)

Chili Hot Beans, like all legumes are packed with energy and are extremely low in fat - just a tiny trace. Since the Mexican flavor is popular with so many people, including me, this is a great bean to use for that unique Mexican taste.

I like to use Bush's Chili Hot Beans when I make chili, and I also use them to top a baked potato. See the recipes on pages 79, 89, and 93.

FOR EXTRA FLAVOR: If you like the Mexican flavor, add salsa or picante sauce to your beans. My favorite brand is Pace. If you want just a bit of the Mexican flavor, use the "mild" variety. If you want your tongue on fire, use "hot".

OATMEAL 6

My Choice: Quaker Old Fashioned

This may be one of our very best grain choices. When we talk about health, fiber, ease of digestion and high energy, we really have a winner here. This is my husband's favorite cereal, but you ought to see the way he eats it. To start with, he only cooks it for about 15 seconds in boiling water. (That's right, he cooks it. He won't let me prepare it.) After it's cooked, he adds concentrated apple juice for sweetener, then he adds a heaping tablespoon of wheat germ and a handful of raisins. Since he doesn't want milk to ruin a good thing, he adds water.

I'll have to admit, you can't put much more energy in a cereal bowl, and it tastes great. The fruit taste from the apple juice concentrate and the raisins really sets it off. If you're not eating oatmeal now, I encourage you to rediscover this exceptional high energy and almost no-fat food. If you don't like it mushy, don't let it cook so long.

I know one person who eats it like cold cereal. She just adds milk. And oatmeal isn't just for breakfast anymore. Eat it like a snack.

FOR SWEETENING: Use apple juice concentrate (see page 17).

FOR CRUNCH & FLAVOR: Try Kretschmer Wheat Germ. Are you one of the many people who has never tried wheat germ? If so, you're not alone. Many people have never eaten wheat germ. It is very tasty as well as nutritious. It has a wonderful nutty flavor, and this is why I like to serve it on top of yogurt - either the frozen or refrigerated varieties. Wheat germ is an excellent source of protein, fiber, B vitamins, iron, selenium and vitamin E. Two tablespoons of wheat germ supply us with half the vitamin E the USRDA says we need in a day. I always add wheat germ to muffins, pancakes, waffles, biscuits, cookies, oatmeal etc. I encourage you to add wheat germ to your grocery list. Just refrigerate it after it has been opened.

Wheat germ is not lowfat. It is 27% fat, which is under the 30% recommended by many health organizations, but in my books 27% is high. But because a small amount of wheat germ is such a powerhouse of nutrients and energy, it is important to include it in our foods.

7 REFRIED BEANS
My Choice: Rosarita, No Fat

Many people think refried beans are high in fat, and they can be. It's usually in restaurants where we find high fat refried beans because the chef adds extra fat to the canned beans. Refried beans, right out of the can, usually are not high in fat. Rosarita, No Fat Refried Beans is truly a fat free, high energy food.

The biggest complaint I hear about beans is that they cause gas. It's true they do - if you're not accustomed to eating them. Eating beans is like everything else - start gradually. Eat only a tablespoon or two at a time, then gradually increase the amount until you can eat all you want. If you eat beans only a few times a year, you will have gas. It's guaranteed!

Enjoy refried beans. Use them in dips, as a side dish, for making burritos, chalupas, soft tacos and much more.

WHAT TO USE WITH REFRIED BEANS: Picante sauce! I always mix Pace "Hot" Picante Sauce in my refried beans. (I like really hot Mexican food!) Then I dip in some corn tortilla chips - see page 38 and have a feast!

POTATO (Irish) 8

If I were forced to rank foods for energy, I believe the potato would go at the top of the list. What's really ironic is that nearly all my life (the years I had a weight problem) the potato was one food I was told I certainly couldn't eat. Everyone knew that potatoes made us fat! How wrong we were. I'll guarantee you, we can eat all the baked potatoes we want, everyday, and we will not gain weight. We just need to be very careful what we put on potatoes. (Butter and sour cream are out, but let's look at what we can use; fresh chives, green onions, salsa, beans, soups, nonfat yogurt, fat free cottage cheese and all sorts of spices. Try the recipes on pages 53, 71, and 89.)

Other high fat potato choices we need to avoid include fried potatoes, potato chips and all the creative versions of fried potatoes such as the "tots" etc.

Did you know that you can eat 298 baked potatoes and get less fat than in one 31/2 ounce prime rib!! Care to guess which choice would give us the most energy?

POTATO TOPPERS: If you're accustomed to eating butter and sour cream on your potato, use Butter Buds or Molly McButter.

It is difficult for me to believe that these products do not contain additives or preservatives. But they are high in sodium.

9   SWEET POTATO

Sweet potatoes are absolutely packed with energy and fiber, and fat is nonexistent - unless we add it. Sweet potatoes come in different colors, anywhere from white to orange to a purplish red. The orange colored varieties are highest in beta carotene, a powerful antioxidant.

American yams and sweet potatoes have the same food value, but not so for tropical yams. Tropical yams have no beta carotene. Most all yams we see in our supermarkets are American yams. If you're not sure which kind your store has, ask the produce person if the yams are American.

There is no comparison between an oven-baked sweet potato, or yam, and one that is microwave-baked. The oven-baked is so moist and sweet, and I can assure you that you will not need to add anything to it, only a little pepper and salt if you'd like.

Don't have time to bake sweet potatoes in the oven? Well, bake a big batch on the weekend, eat what you want when they're baked, then after the leftovers are cool, put them in a container and refrigerate. During the week when you want a sweet potato, just slice or chunk it into a pot, add a bit of water and heat till warm.

When these power packed foods are in season, enjoy them often.

SWEET POTATO TOPPERS: If you just "have" to add butter to your sweet potato, use either Butter Buds or Molly McButter.

If you like candied sweet potatoes, use apple juice concentrate in place of the usual sweetener. (Add some raisins, too.)

WINTER SQUASH   **10**

What is winter squash? Winter squashes are the ones that take a long time to cook - because they are complex carbohydrates. They are filled with energy and fiber and have no fat. The winter squashes include butternut, hubbard, spaghetti and acorn. (Pumpkin belongs to this family as well.)

Just so you will know, summer squashes include zucchini, scallop and yellow crookneck. These squashes cook very quickly because they are simple carbohydrate vegetables, but are not energy packed like the winter squashes; however, they contain valuable vitamins and minerals which we need.

Winter squashes are also good sources of beta carotene, but nothing like sweet potatoes, American yams or pumpkin.

I like to cut acorn squashes in half, scoop out the seeds, invert on a plate and microwave till done. These are very tasty - and quick to fix. Add just a little salt and pepper, and you have a scrumptious, high energy food.

SEASONINGS: If you like the buttery taste, use Butter Buds or Molly McButter along with a bit of salt and pepper.

Try eating vegetables plain to get the "real" taste of the food. If this doesn't turn your taste buds on, use seasonings.

11 CORN

Corn is one of those wonderful foods that I was told years ago to stay away from if I wanted to lose weight. How wrong "diets" were back then! Corn is a high energy, lowfat, complex carbohydrate that is certainly on my "eat list" now.

We can buy fresh corn, frozen corn and canned corn. However, canned corn is not the best choice.

Corn is a grain, and as such, makes a perfect complete protein combination with legumes. This is why beans and corn bread, as well as refried beans and tortilla chips, make wonderful meals.

Add corn to your shopping list, and add it to soups and stews and to vegetable salads - or eat it on the cob. (Just don't add butter - enjoy the true taste of the corn.) If you are accustomed to eating corn with butter, gradually cut down on the amount you use until you can enjoy corn without the taste of fat.

Want to try something a little different? If you have the opportunity, eat just-picked-corn raw. If you have never tried it, don't turn up your nose. It is fantastic! It is good raw only when you pick it right off the stalk.

SEASONINGS: As you can tell, I like my veggies plain - without seasonings. But if you like the buttery taste, use Molly McButter or Butter Buds.

There are some spices that are wonderful combinations of herbs, with no salt. Mrs. Dash has a wide variety as does Natural Blend & Parsley Patch. Experiment and see which you like best.

PEAS   12

This is another of those wonderful foods that I was told I couldn't eat if I wanted to lose weight. I get angry when I think of all the foods I did without for years because I was always on a "diet". I didn't eat bread, potatoes, corn or peas. This is absolutely ridiculous! I'll tell you what, I'm making up for lost time and enjoying every minute of it. The greatest thing is that I never think about my weight now. I am trim and healthy, and I'm enjoying life, and food - the right kinds.

Peas are complex carbohydrates, which means they are high energy, lowfat foods. They are also legumes, thus they are an excellent protein combination with grains including corn. See the recipe on page 61.

Peas are great to add to soups, stews, casseroles, pasta salads and vegetable salads. Fresh or frozen are the best choices. Use them every chance you get.

SEASONINGS: For the buttery taste, use Molly McButter or Butter Buds.

SALAD DRESSING: Salad dressings can be a real problem because so many are high in fat or sugar.

The dressings I use for vegetable salads and pasta salads are Good Seasons Fat Free Dressings: Italian, Honey Mustard, Zesty Herb & Creamy Italian. These dressings truly are fat free, but they are very high in sodium. For lower sodium, either dilute the dressing with water or use a small amount of dressing.

For a creamy dressing, mix plain, nonfat yogurt into the dressing. (I add a minced garlic clove to most salad dressings.)

13 CORN MEAL & CORN BREAD MIX

My Choice: Arrowhead Mills, Hodgson Mill

For those of us who like to make our own corn bread and corn meal muffins from "scratch", I recommend Arrowhead Mills and Hodgson Mill corn meal. Both are made of 100% yellow corn meal with nothing taken out or nothing added.

Degerminated corn meal, such as Quaker Corn Meal, has to be enriched to put back into the product some of what has been taken out. It is enriched only with these nutrients: niacin, iron, thiamine, riboflavin, and folacin. Obviously, other nutrients are destroyed, but only these five are replaced.

Just a note: Since bugs know a good thing when they smell it, if you don't plan using the whole grain corn meal right away, store it in the refrigerator or freezer. By contrast, degerminated corn meal will keep for years at room temperature. The life is taken out of it!

What about corn bread mix?

My Choice: Arrowhead Mills Corn Bread Mix

Many of us don't want to take the time to make corn bread from "scratch". This is why I keep Arrowhead Mills Corn Bread Mix on hand - it's so quick and easy. Corn bread is a very high energy, lowfat food - if we don't add butter, that is.

Most corn bread mixes are made with degerminated cornmeal - but not these. Because whole corn meal mix will not set on the shelf forever, keep it in the refrigerator or freezer.

Keep corn bread mix on hand to fix with your next pot of beans, or soup, or to have with most any meal. Your family will praise you!

WHAT TO PUT ON CORNBREAD: As you probably suspect, I don't put butter on my corn bread. But years ago I used a lot of butter. I gradually cut down the amount until now, I don't use any. I prefer the taste of the corn bread by itself.

If you use butter, I suggest that you gradually cut down. You might try using apple butter or an all fruit jam in place of the butter. For the brands to use, see page 20.

BULGUR-TABOLI WHEAT 14
My Choice: Steakhouse

There are various spellings for taboli, as well as bulgur; tabbouleh and bulghur are a couple. Taboli salad is made of bulgur. Bulgur is cracked wheat that has been partially cooked and then toasted. Bulgur cooks in a very short time, and it will also soften simply by letting it set in water.

Because the wheat berries have both the bran and germ, bulgur is a powerhouse when it comes to nutrients, fiber and energy.

There are many brands of bulgur on the market. Most supermarkets display their bulgur in the produce department. If you don't find it, just ask.

Most all taboli salad is very high in fat, but not my recipe. Give it a try and see what you think. I hope you enjoy it as much as my family does. See recipe on page 73.

BARLEY 15
My Choice: Quaker

Barley is a grain that we don't see used often. I don't know why this is. Maybe after you give it a try, you will find it on your table more often.

Whole barley has an indigestible outer hull. Pearled barley has this outer hull removed to reduce the cooking time. Quick pearled barley cooks even faster because it has been flattened by rollers. In fact, it resembles whole, rolled oats. It takes only 10 minutes to cook the quick variety.

Barley has the same high energy and the almost no fat characteristics of the other grains, and it offers a new taste. Try the recipe on page 75, and see what you think.

16 WHOLE WHEAT FLOUR
My Choice: Arrowhead Mills, Gold Medal, Hodgson Mill and Pillsbury

WHOLE WHEAT PASTRY FLOUR
My Choice: Arrowhead Mills

Let's talk about both of these fantastic products together since they are so similar. The only difference between them is, whole wheat pastry flour is made from soft wheat and is ground for a fine-textured finished product, while regular whole wheat flour is made from hard wheat. Both are made by using the entire whole wheat berry. This includes the outside bran layer and the germ, as well as the starchy endosperm.

Hard wheat is high in gluten - this is the protein that is elastic and responds to yeast in bread baking. Gluten is what causes light, airy loaves of bread. If we use regular whole wheat flour in unyeasted baked goods such as biscuits, pancakes, muffins, cookies, etc., they will be somewhat dense and heavy. Many people like this kind of texture. If you like yours lighter, just use whole wheat pastry flour.

Whole wheat pastry flour, made from soft wheat, is lower in gluten. Just remember, if you want a light texture in foods that do not require yeast, use whole wheat pastry flour. But for foods with yeast, use regular whole wheat flour.

Whether we use regular whole wheat or whole wheat pastry flour, both are very high energy, lowfat foods filled with vitamins, minerals and fiber. In all your baking, use either of these. As soon as you finish your bleached or unbleached stuff, stock your pantry with whole wheat. You'll feel great about giving your family these high quality foods.

ADD CRUNCH TO BAKED GOODS WITH: Sunflower kernels. Sunflower kernels, or nuts, are absolutely wonderful. These little morsels are packed with vitamins, minerals, fiber and protein. You may be picturing the sunflower kernels that are at the end of salad bars. I'm not talking about these! These have been fried in fat, are coated with salt, and have MSG!

UGH! In fact, many of the sunflower kernels on our grocery shelves are the very same. But there are some that are dry roasted or raw. Raw is the best choice as these kernels have more nutrients than the dry roasted. Unfortunately many supermarkets do not carry raw kernels, only the dry roasted. However, most all health food stores carry raw sunflower kernels. If you are not fortunate enough to have a grocery store that carries raw kernels, look for a health food store, and stock up on these little gems. I keep a jar of kernels handy in the refrigerator and freeze the rest until I'm ready to use them.

Sunflower kernels are also very high in fat. In fact, they're 78% fat. Because they are so nutritious and packed with energy, we should eat them, but not go overboard. I add them to salads, pancakes, waffles, biscuits, muffins, cookies, on top of yogurt, etc.

17 MUFFIN MIXES

My Choice: Arrowhead Mills and Hodgson Mill

I like to make muffins from "scratch", but there are occasions when I just don't want to take the time, so I'll grab a box of muffin mix.

There are a few brands of good, high energy, lowfat muffins on the market. Among them are; Arrowhead Mills, Hodgson Mill and Hain. I use either Arrowhead Mills or Hodgson Mill then I "doctor it up" by adding raisins, wheat germ and chopped nuts or seeds.

So many muffins and snack-cake type snacks are made with energy and nutrient deficient white flour with lots of fat and highly processed sugar. These foods rob us of energy and add fat to the waistline.

It is so easy to whip up a batch of high energy, lowfat muffins from a mix. If you have children, let them help you make the muffins. They will have fun doing it, and they will enjoy the muffins more when they have helped make them. (See if you can get them to help clean up the mess, too!)

"DOCTOR THEM UP" WITH: Sliced almonds.

Do you like nuts but won't eat them because they are so high in fat? It is true, nuts are high in fat. But the good news is that we must have some fat in our diet. In fact there is one fat that we must eat for good health. It is called linoleic acid. Doesn't sound like a fat, does it? It is, and it is absolutely essential that we get it daily. The only place we can get linoleic acid is from plant foods, and nuts and seeds are the best sources.

As I said, nuts are high in fat. Almonds are 74% fat. They are also great sources of bone-building nutrients (calcium & magnesium), iron, zinc, fiber, and they contain many other valuable nutrients.

When buying any nuts or seeds, buy only the raw varieties. Many packaged nuts are toasted in oil, and some even have seasonings with additives and preservatives.

It is important to include nuts and seeds in our diet, we just don't want to go overboard.

BISCUIT MIX 18
My Choice: Arrowhead Mills

This is another super, high energy, lowfat mix for the busy person. I don't know anyone who doesn't like biscuits, but unless you really like to cook and have the time, you're not going to make biscuits from "scratch".

(You know those biscuits we see in the refrigerated section of our stores? I don't even consider these food! They are made with highly processed flour and are absolutely loaded with additives and preservatives.)

I use Arrowhead Mills Multi Grain Biscuit Mix. The recipe on the package says to use 1/4 cup oil, but I use only 2 TB oil and add 2 TB water.

Did you know that you can really give some "zip" to your biscuits by adding spices? Try Italian seasoning or a bit of dill or celery seed, or chopped onion. Be creative.

WHAT TO PUT ON A BISCUIT: I like my biscuits without anything added to them, but if you like something sweet, use an all-fruit jam such as Smucker's Simply Fruit, or any of the other brands listed on page 20. Try to do without adding butter.

19 PANCAKE & WAFFLE MIXES
My Choice: Arrowhead Mills

Pancake and waffle mixes are so convenient for those hearty weekend breakfasts. But who's to say we should eat pancakes only for breakfast anyway! Have them anytime. If you don't want to make yours from "scratch", just use a mix that is made with whole grains such as Arrowhead Mills Multi Grain. It contains whole wheat, whole corn, brown rice and whole rye flours.

Pancakes or waffles made from a mix like this are just "bustin" with energy, and they're lowfat. I always add a little extra nutrition, and crunch, to my pancakes. I throw in about 1/4 cup raw sunflower kernels, sliced almonds, or chopped pecans to a batch of pancakes or waffles.

I like to make extra waffles to freeze, so all I have to do is put them in the toaster for a quick breakfast during the week.

If you prefer syrup, use the real stuff. The ones I use are Old Colony and Cary's Real Maple Syrup. Only real maple syrup is acceptable. All others are imposters made from very highly processed sugars with additives and preservatives.

I remember one Saturday morning walking into a restaurant that featured whole grain foods. In clear view was this gentleman sitting at a table eating the largest stack of pancakes I had ever seen. They looked 12 inches across and were stacked 4 inches high! Not realizing, I must have stopped and stared at him, because he looked up and said, "What's the matter, lady? Haven't you ever seen someone eat pancakes?" My response was, "Yes, but never so many. How do you keep from getting fat?" Do you know what he said? "If you eat the right foods, you'll never get fat, regardless of how much you eat."

That was probably ten years ago that this happened, and it didn't take me long to figure out what he was talking about. Since then, I have sat down to some pretty big meals myself, and it sure feels good knowing that I won't walk away a fatter person.

WHAT TO PUT ON TOP: Try heated apple juice concentrate. This is very sweet, and nutritious as well. Or try any of the all-fruit jams such as Simply Fruit by Smuckers. These have no refined sugars in them.

BOXED DINNERS 20
My Choice: Pritikin

Normally I don't have anything good to say about boxed dinners, but Pritikin Dinners are excellent. They have two varieties; Oriental Dinner and Mexican Dinner. To make these a complete meal just add a can of beans or a small amount of chicken, turkey or shrimp. I always add steamed vegetables on the side, such as broccoli, cabbage, cauliflower, etc.

These Pritikin Dinners are made with high energy brown rice and they're very low in fat. I keep Pritikin Dinners in my pantry for those days when I'm especially lazy.

Nearly every supermarket carries Pritikin products. If yours doesn't have these dinners, ask for them.

CANNED SOUPS 21
With whole grains, beans, or potatoes
My Choice: Health Valley

There are some wonderful, hearty, high energy, fat free, canned soups by Health Valley on our grocery shelves. All the grains used in Health Valley canned soups are whole grains - the rice is brown rice, and the noodles are made with whole wheat. No highly processed grains in these soups, and there's no fat! Can't beat a deal like this!

I like to keep these soups on hand for a really quick meal when I don't want to take the time to cook. One of my favorite soups is Real Italian Minestrone.

Unfortunately most of the soups on our grocery shelves wouldn't impress Grandma! Most have highly processed ingredients with fat and lots of sodium added - but not these canned soups by Health Valley. Grandma would be proud!

22 CORN TORTILLAS & TORTILLA CHIPS

My Choice: Our House, Del Sol, Jimenez, and Orbit

Soft corn tortillas are one of my favorite foods, and it seems that most everyone enjoys corn tortillas. I like to warm them in the microwave, roll them up, then dip them in salsa. By the way, when you eat in a Mexican restaurant, ask for soft corn tortillas to dip in your salsa instead of the fried variety that comes at the start of every meal. (Just be sure the cook hasn't added fat to the soft tortilla!)

At home I use corn tortillas to make soft tacos, chalupas, burritos, enchiladas, etc. Be creative, and enjoy this wonderful, high energy, lowfat food.

JUST A NOTE: There are many brands of locally produced tortillas. Choose those made only of corn, water and lime. (Since tortillas are treated with lime, they're a good source of absorbable calcium.)

What about the tortilla chips?

My Choice: Guiltless Gourmet

Guiltless Gourmet makes wonderful high energy, lowfat, great tasting chips.

I must quote to you from the bag. "Guiltless Gourmet chips are baked, not fried, and contain only four ingredients - corn, water, lime and salt in the salted variety. Therefore, when you eat a Guiltless Gourmet chip, you get the real, fresh, crunchy taste of corn, not a big dollop of preservative filled grease on top of a soaked and saturated glob of corn too battered to even cry out for help." I couldn't have said it better!!

Read on: "When you pick up (Guiltless Gourmet chips), you're holding a bag of honest corn tortilla chips. A bag of fried chips owes up to 35% of its weight to oil and over 50% of its calories to fat. Yuk! That's not what you want to get in return for your hard-earned cash. In a 7 ounce bag of Guiltless Gourmet chips, you usually get as many chips as you will find in a 10 ounce bag of the other guys' chips, because the weight is not taken up by oil."

These chips are one of my favorite snacks. Wonderful flavor and crunch!

FOLLOWING ARE EIGHT OF MY FAVORITE READY-MADE SNACK FOODS. MOST SNACK FOODS ARE A DISASTER FOR WEIGHT CONTROL, BUT NOT THESE EIGHT CHOICES. THEY ARE ALL HIGH ENERGY, LOWFAT AND NUTRITIOUS. AND THEY TASTE GOOD TOO!

CRACKERS 23

My Choice: Health Valley, RYVITA, Kavli, Finn Crisp

Crackers can be a terrible choice if we do not know what we're looking for; however, if crackers are made with whole grains with no fat or additives or preservatives, they are an excellent energy food. There are four brands that I really enjoy and think are great. They are: Health Valley, RYVITA, Kavli and Finn Crisp. All of these crackers are great for snacks and with soup or salads. They are also easy to keep with you in the car or slip into your desk at work.

WHAT TO SPREAD ON A CRACKER: Do you like cream cheese on a cracker? "Real" cream cheese is very high in fat. In fact, it is higher in fat than any other cheese. But you can make your own cream cheese that is fat free and tastes wonderful.

Put a carton of plain, nonfat yogurt in a small-holed colander. Place it over a bowl and let set in the refrigerator for a couple days - until all the excess liquid drains off. (If you stir the yogurt ever so often, it will drain faster.)

Now you have a semi-solid yogurt that tastes remarkably like cream cheese - but without the fat!

24 POPCORN

My Choice: Raw kernels only, all brands

When we think about it, popcorn has to be one of the most original and unique foods available. Popcorn has to rate as the king of all snack foods. I don't feel there is a week that goes by that I don't fix a batch or two of popcorn. It is great finger food - very rich in energy and very low in fat.

We Americans, however, have tried to ruin a high energy food. We have added fat, fat, fat in the form of cooking oil and butter (sometimes cheese) and lots of salt until a good, healthful food has become a health hazard! Folks, this just won't work. We need to rediscover the "real" taste of popcorn. The only, and I emphasize "only", way popcorn should be eaten is plain with nothing added. It took me about two weeks to get used to the taste of real popcorn, and now just the thought of the buttered, greasy stuff turns my stomach!

25 BREAD STICKS

My Choice: Whole wheat by Gardetto's, Angonoa's, Oroweat

Do you like something crunchy for an afternoon snack? Do you like crackers with your soup or salad? Then give these whole wheat breadsticks a try. These are not only crunchy, they are satisfying and packed with energy and fiber.

Most breadsticks are made with that nutrient and energy deficient white flour and have additives and preservatives - but not these.

One thing about breadsticks, they're so small they can easily be tucked in a purse or briefcase and go right with you for a quick snack when the hungries hit. Also, take them with you to eat with soup or a salad.

PRETZELS 26

My Choice: Whole wheat by Barbara's or Wege

Pretzels make great snacks. Snacks can be our downfall, or they can be a great pick-me-up. Most snacks are swimming in fat, are made with highly processed flour and sugar, and contain additives and preservatives. But these pretzels, by either Barbara's or Wege, are made with whole wheat - organic whole wheat at that - so they are satisfying, energy filled, and they are fat free. They also satisfy that urge to "crunch".

I keep a few in a zip lock bag and take with me when I'm on the road - in a car or plane.

As always, if your favorite store doesn't have these, they can get them.

A TASTE TREAT: Dip pretzels in plain, nonfat yogurt. I certainly think this tastes good. Give it a try.

FOOD FOR THOUGHT

Always remember, when I use the expression, "Never Go Hungry," I mean it. When we're hungry, this means our motor is running and our fuel tank is on "E". This says we'd better look for some quality fuel, and things like these quality snacks are premium fuel that give us energy. A snack can pick us up and give us energy, or it can pull us down and add the pounds. It's our choice!

27 FRUIT BARS
My Choice: Health Valley

There are some wonderful fruit bars by Health Valley. The varieties are Apricot, Date, Raisin & Apple. These bars are made with organic whole grains, fruits and fruit juices. They make a truly nutritious breakfast or snack. They're packed with vitamins, minerals, fiber, and complex carbohydrates. They're loaded with energy, and they're Fat Free. Can't beat a snack like this!

These bars are individually wrapped which makes them easy to toss in a lunch bag or in a briefcase. Add these to your shopping list for those times when you're rushed for breakfast, or for a pick-me-up in the afternoon.

28 BANANA

Generally, fruits and vegetables are not considered complex carbohydrates (high energy foods). But I don't care what the textbooks say, in my opinion, the banana is an exception and is a good energy food. It works that way for me and many others. I nearly always have bananas available and eat them mainly as a snack when I feel a hunger pang or need a little pick-me-up. I also add them to cereal and use them in a fruit salad. They are also an excellent snack for children - and children just love them.

Be creative with bananas, and give this a try. Get some slightly overripe bananas, peel them and put them separately in Baggies, then freeze. Now, when the children come in for a snack, offer them one of these frozen guys. I'll guarantee you, they'll love them. They eat just like a popsicle - but oh so much better!

COOKIES 29
My Choice: Health Valley

Now I'm sure you will think I've lost my marbles because everyone knows that if anything will put on the pounds it's cookies. And 99% of the time, cookies are a bad choice because most are made with highly processed flour and sugars. But here we have something unique. Just look at the ingredient list:

Organic 100% whole wheat Organic oats
All natural pineapple, pear and apple juice

And each cookie has 3 grams of fiber. This is fantastic!

We can definitely upgrade the quality of our snacks and our children's snacks with cookies like these. Health Valley offers many varieties of Fat Free Cookies. These cookies are not only great snacks, they are great for breakfast on those mornings when we, or the kids, are running behind. Some of these cookies with a glass of orange juice make a very good breakfast. (Your kids will look at you in amazement when you tell them to have some cookies for breakfast!)

GRANOLA BARS 30
My Choice: Health Valley

Health Valley makes several varieties of high energy, Fat Free, Granola Bars. Each variety is very tasty, and they're made with whole grains only. Each bar is individually wrapped and easy to take to work or school.

I hear so many people say they don't have time for breakfast. With these Granola Bars, there's nothing to do - just eat and then run - or eat while on the run!

THE "FABULOUS 30" RECIPES

This recipe is for all the Mexican food lovers out there - and this includes me. The problem we have with this tasty food is: How can we make it taste good without the fat?

ARROZ CON POLLO   1
Makes 6 servings

3/4 pound boneless, skinless chicken breast,
    cut into thin strips
1/2 tsp. cumin
1/2 tsp. chili powder
2 tsp. sunflower oil
1 small onion, chopped
1 garlic clove, minced
1 can (14 1/2 oz) tomatoes
1/3 cup picante sauce (Pace)
1 cup hot water
2 cups INSTANT BROWN RICE (Uncle Ben's)
1 can (8 oz) KIDNEY BEANS, drained (S&W)

Heat oil in skillet; sprinkle chicken with cumin & chili powder; sauté chicken 2 to 3 minutes. Add onion & garlic; stir. Add tomatoes, water & picante sauce; heat to boiling. Add rice; reduce heat; cover & simmer 5 minutes. Stir in beans. Let set, covered, 3 minutes, for all liquid to absorb.

Add a steamed vegetable such as broccoli or cauliflower, or make a salad. If you use salad dressing, use a very small amount.

Personally, I like my Mexican food fairly spicy, so I use a bit more chili powder, and cumin as well. Of course, you can use a mild or hot picante sauce to change the "temperature" of this dish.

You can purchase chicken already skinned, boned and cut into thin strips. This is more expensive than preparing your own, but it definitely saves time.

If you are concerned about your sodium intake, purchase no-salt tomatoes and rinse the kidney beans. The only thing left that contains sodium is the picante sauce.

This is one of my family's favorite meals. I hope yours likes it, too.

ARROZ CON POLLO

Per Serving:

Calories: 285   Sodium: 335 mg

Fat: 5 g   Fiber: 4 g

TIDBIT...

WOW! CHIPS

You've probably seen these chips made with Olestra (Olean). Here is the warning label on these chips:

> *This Product Contains Olestra.* Olestra may cause abdominal cramping and loose stools. Olestra inhibits the absorption of some vitamins and other nutrients. Vitamins A, D, E, and K have been added.

Why are vitamins A, D, E, and K added? You see, Olestra takes these fat-soluble vitamins right out of our bodies. (Who knows what else Olestra takes out as well!!) These are extremely valuable nutrients that will not be absorbed because of Olestra.

I think this is of greater concern than abdominal cramping and loose stools. We will know if we have these problems! But we won't know how much of these valuable nutrients are being depleted.

Vitamins A and E are powerful antioxidants. They help build a strong immune system. Vitamin D is essential for normal growth and development of bones and teeth - especially in children. Vitamin D is important in the prevention of osteoporosis. Vitamin K is essential for blood clotting. Without adequate Vitamin K, we can bleed to death.

Do you like pizza? Who doesn't! Why not have a pizza sandwich? Pack one (or two) in your, or your child's, lunch.

Make your shopping list now for this great tasting meal. This sandwich fills you up so you won't be hungry a couple hours after eating. Most everyone will like this taste because it has a mild pizza flavor - but without all the fat of pizza.

PIZZA SANDWICH   2
Makes 1 serving

2 slices WHOLE WHEAT BREAD
1/4 cup shredded low moisture, part skim
  mozzarella cheese
2 TB spaghetti sauce *(Healthy Choice)*

Toast the bread; sprinkle a thin layer of shredded mozzarella cheese on one slice. Drop spaghetti sauce on the cheese; top with another thin layer of cheese; then add the second piece of toast. Put in a Baggie, and now all you have to do is wait for lunch!

Also eat fresh veggies; carrot sticks, cauliflower, green or red pepper, etc. Also have a pear or an apple and a couple of cookies. Health Valley Fat Free cookies are great.

FOOD FOR THOUGHT

All recipes in *15 MINUTE STORAGE MEALS* are planned around complex carbohydrates (energy foods), not around meat as most American meals are. I know that it is difficult to change our thought process to: "What kind of complex carbohydrate will I fix for dinner?" instead of "What kind of meat am I going to have for dinner?" But we need to think in terms of planning the entire meal around such foods as potatoes, sweet potatoes, brown rice, whole wheat pasta, legumes, whole grains, etc. These are the foods that are very low in fat, no cholesterol, very low in sodium and high in energy and fiber. These foods contain the "good stuff" we need for good health and weight control.

PIZZA SANDWICH

Per Serving:

Calories: 290	*Sodium: 710 mg*
Fat: 8 g	*Fiber: 4.25 g*

TIDBIT...

SHOULD WE BE CONCERNED WITH HEART DISEASE?

If you are young, active, or seem to be healthy, it may be difficult to be concerned about heart disease. But a build-up of plaque (fatty deposits on artery walls) has been found in children as young as four years of age!

Researchers feel that plaque at this young age is due mainly to fast foods; those in restaurants as well as those at home. In our fast-paced society, it's easy to have handy such foods as frankfurters, cheese, peanut butter and whole milk. If foods like this are eaten regularly, fatty deposits can build up on artery walls.

Did you know that cardiovascular disease kills an American every 32 <u>seconds!</u> These statistics tell of just those who die, not those who have heart attacks, strokes, etc. and live.

Probably all of us can do something about these alarming statistics. We can eat more fresh fruits and vegetables, <u>whole</u> grains and legumes. When we eat more of these foods, we simply don't have room for other, unhealthy foods.

This dish is like a goulash - the vegetables and meat cook together. I like to prepare meals this way, then I don't have to cook vegetables as a side dish.

SICILIAN PASTA **3**
Makes 6 servings

4 cups boiling water
3 cups WHOLE WHEAT PASTA

1/2 pound ground white turkey
1 medium onion, chopped
2 garlic cloves, minced
2 TB WHOLE WHEAT FLOUR
8 oz fresh mushrooms, coarsely chopped
1 large green pepper (use the seeds)
2 cans (14 1/2 oz) tomatoes
1/2 cup spaghetti sauce *(Healthy Choice)*
2 TB Italian seasoning

The key to getting this meal to the table quickly is to put a pot of hot water on to boil right away. As soon as it boils, put in the pasta. You can use any kind of whole wheat pasta, but I like macaroni. While the pasta simmers for 10 minutes, do the following:

Brown the turkey with the onion and garlic; stir in the flour; chop the mushrooms and green pepper in your hands and add to the mixture; stir in the tomatoes, the spaghetti sauce and the Italian seasoning, and simmer.

You can either serve the sauce over the pasta, or combine the pasta and sauce. Serve it however you think your family will enjoy it best.

I like to have a piece of whole wheat bread with this meal.

SICILIAN PASTA

Per Serving:

Calories: 300   *Sodium: 320 mg*

Fat: 2.5 g   *Fiber: 8.6 g*

TIDBIT...

SPORTS DRINKS

Most sports drinks consist primarily of sugar-water and artificial colors. There are very small amounts of potassium and sodium (electrolytes) added to these sports drinks. What most people want in sports drinks are the electrolytes lost when they perspire. Gatorade, as an example, has 110mg sodium and only 30mg potassium. Not much at all!

There is a *much* better choice. In fact there are two choices. We can make our own sports drinks by adding a bit of salt to fruit or veggie juices OR we can drink V8 Juice.

An 8oz glass (1 cup) of orange juice has 480mg of potassium and 25mg of sodium. By adding only 1/8 teaspoon salt, we add 290mg of extra sodium. Now, we have a wonderful sports drink with nutritious ingredients, no refined sugar or artificial colors!

How about V8 Juice? V8 is made from a variety of vegetables with no sugar or artificial colors. A 5.5oz can has 380mg of potassium and 430mg of sodium. What a simple, nutritious way to get electrolytes!

(For more info about juices to use as sports drinks, see page 54.)

Want a quick, easy, hearty, lowfat lunch? Try this one. Most all offices are equipped with a microwave, can opener, and a refrigerator, so you can take the fixin's to work with you. If you fix lunch at home for yourself or for your children, this one is a snap.

SPUDS & MORE
Makes 1 serving

4

1 medium potato
1 cup Beef Vegetable Soup *(Healthy Choice)*

Bake potato in the microwave until done. Put potato on a microwaveable plate, split in half, and mash it a bit. Top with the soup. Place back in the microwave and heat until the soup is warm. (Put the leftover soup in a container in the fridge to eat later.) What could be simpler?

Like most all soups, Healthy Choice is high in sodium, but when it is added to a potato (which has virtually no salt) the entire meal is low in sodium.

This can be a very good evening meal for the family. You just need to allow extra time for more potatoes to cook.

This is a very lowfat meal that is high in vitamins, minerals, fiber, and complex carbohydrates. The CCs (complex carbohydrates) are what give us energy for our muscles as well as for brain power.

I think you'll enjoy not only how good this meal tastes, but also how quick it is to fix. Just keep these two simple ingredients on hand, and you have a nutritious meal in no time.

FOOD FOR THOUGHT

What happens when we're driving down the road and we lift up on the accelerator? Our car slows down, doesn't it? The same thing happens to the body when we don't feed it. And what is our fuel? The energy foods. Keep your tank on full, using the "Fabulous 30" foods.

SPUDS & MORE

Per Serving:

Calories: 350   *Sodium: 435 mg*

Fat: 1.2 g   *Fiber: 5.6 g*

TIDBIT...

SPORTS DRINKS, cont.

Here are some great juice choices that can be used as sports drinks. Let's look at these juices and the milligrams of potassium in 8 ounces (1 cup):

JUICE	POTASSIUM
Grape	335
Pineapple	335
Grapefruit	374
Orange-grapefruit	390
Orange	480
Tomato	535
Prune	705

These truly are healthful choices for potassium. Now for a TRUE sports drink, add 1/8 teaspoon salt to each of these juices.

Remember that it's *very* important to drink plenty of water when participating in physical activities, particularly in hot weather. Drink. Drink. Drink water - even though you may not feel thirsty. Then occasionally have one of these good-for-you sports drinks.

This recipe is so quick to fix, and you don't have to cook a thing! Also, this is great to throw together in the morning before going to work, and then it's waiting on you. All you have to do is get out the plates!

QUICK MEXICAN SALAD 5
Makes 6 servings

1 can (15 oz each)
   BLACK BEANS *(Ranch Style)*
   CHILI HOT BEANS *(Bush's)*
   GREAT NORTHERN BEANS *(Bush's)*
   (drain all beans, but do not rinse)
1 large red bell pepper, chopped (use the seeds)
2/3 cup mild salsa *(Pace)*
1/2 cup chopped green onions
1 garlic clove, minced

4 oz shredded, low moisture, part skim mozzarella cheese

Mix the ingredients together - all but the cheese. Serve the shredded mozzarella on the side, and if you want cheese, sprinkle a very small amount on top. That's it! Enjoy!!

This is fantastic served with cornbread. If you don't want to go to the trouble of making cornbread, just serve Guiltless Gourmet Tortilla Chips or some whole grain crackers. Your family will love you for this one, and you'll like it because it's so simple and nutritious.

NOTE: If you need to watch your sodium intake, I would suggest rinsing the canned beans and using just a small amount of salsa.

If you want to change this recipe the next time you fix it, try turkey or chicken instead of the cheese. For a very quick meal, use deli-thin turkey or chicken torn into pieces.

FOOD FOR THOUGHT

We should always plan our meals around the energy foods. A minimum of 50% (more if active) of our food consumption should come from these foods. A minimum of 30% should come from neutral foods (fruits and vegetables) and not over 10% from the fat/processed foods.

QUICK MEXICAN SALAD

Per Serving:

Calories: 260   *Sodium: 825 mg*

Fat: 4.3 g   *Fiber: 11 g*

TIDBIT...

SWEETENER - THE BEST CHOICE

Many, many times I've been asked what sweetener is best to use. People who ask this are wanting to eliminate NutraSweet, Sweet & Low, sugar, etc., but they don't know what to use in place of these.

Personally I use apple juice concentrate in many of my recipes; however, a liquid sweetener isn't always compatible in every recipe. Also, apple juice concentrate wouldn't be very tasty in coffee or tea. So - what to use?

There is a sweetener on the market that is natural *and* healthful. It is called Stevia, and is found in health food stores. Stevia is from a small green plant native to Paraguay. It is about 30 times sweeter than sugar. So - a little goes a long way!!

Unlike artificial sweeteners, Stevia doesn't break down when heated. This makes it an excellent sweetener for cooking and baking.

Is Stevia safe for diabetics? According to James A. May, in "Wisdom of the Ancients", when Stevia is in its pure unadulterated form, it does not adversely affect blood glucose levels and may be used freely by both diabetics and hypoglycemics.

In addition to being very sweet, studies show that Stevia contains vitamins & minerals. What a deal! Stevia is available in liquid and powder form.

NOTE: Purchase **pure** Stevia only. Some varieties of Stevia contain sugar.

Yes, Mexicans eat pasta too. I know many of you like Mexican food but are concerned about all the fat that is in it. These Mexican recipes are excellent and do not have the fat of traditional Mexican dishes.

Mexican dishes normally contain Monterey Jack or cheddar cheese. Both these cheeses are extremely high in fat. This is why I have chosen to use low moisture, part skim mozzarella cheese. Who says we can't change the cheese around a little?

As a side dish, the following recipe doesn't have cheese, but if we want a complete meal, we need to add some cheese, meat, or a complimentary plant food such as legumes. Since most of us are interested in quick, complete meals, that is what this recipe will be.

MEXICAN PASTA   6
Makes 4 servings

3 cups boiling water
2 cups WHOLE WHEAT PASTA

1 can (14 1/2 oz) tomatoes with jalapeños
1 garlic clove, minced
**4 ounces shredded, low moisture, part skim
    mozzarella cheese**

SERVE WITH THIS MEAL:
Fresh or frozen steamed vegetables such as:
Broccoli, carrots cauliflower, green pepper, etc.

Cook the pasta (use whatever shape your family likes) in boiling water for 10 minutes. After it is cooked, drain and then add tomatoes and garlic. Top with cheese.

While the pasta cooks, heat veggies for just a few minutes and serve them as is - no butter. If you're accustomed to the fatty taste, this new taste will be a surprise to you, but you will grow to enjoy the "real" taste of the vegetables.

As you can see, this takes less than 15 minutes to get to the table. Also, these are foods that you can keep on hand to throw together at the last minutes. Enjoy!

MEXICAN PASTA

Per Serving:

Calories: 285   *Sodium: 345 mg*

Fat: 6 g   *Fiber: 6.8 g*

TIDBIT...

JAYNE'S BUTTER MIX

Do you want a great tasting 'butter' for your bread? This is a marvelous tasting spread that tastes just like butter but spreads like margarine.

It is 100% fat, just like butter or margarine; however, it has 1/2 the saturated fat & cholesterol of butter. And it has none of the trans-fatty acids of margarine. (Trans-fats destroy HDLs, "good" cholesterol, and increase LDLs, "bad" cholesterol.)

- 1 pound butter
- 2 cups oil*

Put butter in blender and let set at room temperature until it softens. Add oil, and mix until well blended. Pour into containers and refrigerate. Enjoy!

*I use sunflower oil because it has more vitamin E than most other oils.

I'll have to admit, lowfat Mexican meals rate quite high on my want list. This one, with a bit of Southwest flavor, takes less than 15 minutes to get to the table and tastes wonderful. Can't beat a meal like this!

THE ALBUQUERQUE SPECIAL 7
Makes 4 large servings

1 can (14 1/2 oz) chicken broth (*Swanson, 1/3 Less Sodium*)
2 cups INSTANT BROWN RICE (*Uncle Ben's*)

2 tsp. sunflower oil
1 garlic clove, minced
1 medium onion, chopped
2 small zucchini, thinly sliced

2 cans (14 1/2 oz each) tomatoes
1 can (4 oz) chopped green chilies (*Old El Paso*)

2 oz shredded, low moisture, part skim mozzarella cheese

Bring broth to boil; add rice. Cover and simmer on lowest heat 8 to 10 minutes.

While the rice cooks, sauté garlic and onion in a large skillet; add zucchini and stir. Add tomatoes and green chilies. Heat till bubbly. That's all there is to it!

Serve the zucchini mixture on top of the rice, and then top each serving with just a light sprinkle of shredded mozzarella cheese. (If you want a vegetarian meal, omit the cheese.)

NOTES: If the zucchini mixture is too juicy for you, drain off a bit of the juice. Save it to drink chilled. It's very tasty!

If you use whole canned tomatoes, cut them into chunks while they're simmering in the skillet.

If you need a low sodium dish, use no-salt canned tomatoes. There are some very good choices on the market.

Remember, to save time, chop the onion and slice the zucchini in your hands, and just let them fall into the skillet.

Your family will love you for this meal! If there is any left over, take it to work with you for lunch. (The next time you make this meal, you may want to double the recipe so there will be enough for two meals.)

THE ALBUQUERQUE SPECIAL

Per Serving:

Calories: 315   Sodium: 760 mg

Fat: 6.4 g   Fiber: 4.6 g

TIDBIT...

BREAST CANCER
ON THE RISE IN THE U.S.

There has been a noticeable increase in the rate of breast cancer in the United States since 1940. Why is this happening?

Fruits & Vegetables

We keep hearing over and over how important it is to eat fruits & vegetables *everyday*. (Fresh fruits & vegetables are always the best.)

Researchers note that women from poorer countries, those who routinely eat very little meat and dairy but get most of their foods from plants, have significantly lower rates of breast cancer.

Most all poorer countries have low rates of breast cancer, and their diets consist of fruits, vegetables, legumes and *whole* grains.

• Could it be the fiber in these foods that help protect against cancer?

• Could it be the phytochemicals (plant chemicals) in these foods?

• Could it be the estrogen in these foods?

• What about the myriad of antioxidants present in plant foods? Could they help protect against cancer? I believe it's a combination of all these things.

There's a great side benefit to eating more plant food and less animal and highly processed food. In addition to becoming healthier, if we're overweight, we'll slim down!

Are you in the mood for a cool meal - one that requires no cooking, is very low in fat, takes just a few minutes to prepare and tastes fantastic? Then write down these ingredients NOW and pick them up at your store today! You're familiar with a 'Hole in One'? Well, this is a 'Meal in One'.

VEGETABLE MEDLEY 8
Makes 5 servings

2 cups frozen PEAS
2 cups frozen CORN

2 cups chopped tomatoes
1 cup broccoli florets
1 cup sliced, fresh mushrooms
2 ribs celery, sliced
1/2 cup chopped onion

Shredded, low moisture, part skim mozzarella cheese (optional)

FAT FREE ITALIAN DRESSING

1 cup water
2 TB vinegar
1 garlic clove, minced
1 packet Italian Fat Free Dressing Mix (*Good Seasons*)

Thaw peas and corn at room temperature or in microwave. Prepare remaining vegetable ingredients, and put in a large serving bowl.

Put dressing ingredients in a container with a tight lid. Shake vigorously until well mixed. Add to vegetable mixture and stir. That's it! Enjoy!

This is a complete meal in itself - the peas and corn make a complete protein - but if you want to add a small sprinkling of shredded mozzarella, go ahead. This will give the meal some vitamin B12 - and a small amount of fat.

Try different veggies; red or green bell pepper, zucchini and/ or yellow squash, cucumbers, green onion, cauliflower, etc. (I always use tomatoes as they just 'make' this dish.)

VEGETABLE MEDLEY

Per Serving:

Calories: 130	*Sodium: 65 mg*
Fat: .7 g	*Fiber: 4.5 g*

TIDBIT...

GET A LEG UP ON DIABETES

We know that brisk walking is great for the heart, but a study is telling us that a brisk, 30 minute walk could improve insulin use and help ward off diabetes.

This is great news! In this study reported in the *Journal of the American Medical Association*, researchers found that people who exercise moderately *and* regularly are much less likely to develop diabetes than people who aren't committed to regular, moderate exercise, such as brisk walking.

Sooooooooo, go have a brisk, fun, 30 minute walk!

There must be something wrong - this just tastes too good to be lowfat, nutritious and quick! This is 'Chip & Dip' made into a complete meal. When we think of chips and dip, we automatically think of high fat. Not so in this case. There are some tortilla chips on the market that are made without fat. Of course they're not going to taste like the grease laden varieties but they are very tasty.

A MEXICAN QUICKIE 9
Makes 1 serving

1 serving TORTILLA CHIPS, about 20
(Guiltless Gourmet)
1/2 cup REFRIED BEANS *(Rosarita, No Fat)*
4 TB Picante sauce *(Pace)*

VEGGIES:
Carrot sticks and cauliflower florets

It takes virtually no effort to get this meal together. Just set the bag of chips on the table, open a can of refried beans, put a jar of picante sauce on the table, wash the veggies, and eat!

For all of us Mexican food lovers, this is truly heaven-sent. Besides being so quick and tasting so fabulous, this is very nutritious. It is brimming with energy, with the chips and beans, then the veggies round it out for a complete meal. (Use whatever veggies you like.) If you want to add some grated cheese for vitamin B12, go right ahead. Just be sure that it is a light sprinkling of cheese. (Don't ruin an excellent meal with fat.) Low moisture, part skim mozzarella is a good choice.

Guiltless Gourmet Chips are an excellent source of absorbable calcium because they are processed with lime.

If your store does not carry Guiltless Gourmet, ask for them to be ordered.

FOOD FOR THOUGHT
Diets make you fat. They also make you miserable!

A MEXICAN QUICKIE

Per Serving:

Calories: 250   *Sodium: 1170 mg*

Fat: 1 g   *Fiber: 8 g*

TIDBIT...

VITAMIN E - IN OILS

Which cooking oils are highest in vitamin E? It stands to reason that if the food of origin is high in vitamin E, so will its oil be high in E. Look at the first one on the list!

(One tablespoon is the measure that is used:)

COOKING OIL	MILLIGRAMS
Wheat germ oil	20.30
Sunflower oil	6.10
Almond oil	5.30
Safflower oil	4.60
Corn oil	1.90
Peanut oil	1.60
Olive oil	1.60
Soybean oil	1.50

This is another reason for eating whole wheat foods!! The germ in whole wheat is packed with vitamin E.

It's easy to get more vitamin E. Simply sprinkle wheat germ on your cereal, salads, soups, casseroles, etc.

Another way to get more vitamin E is to add raw sunflower seeds to your salads, etc. Do the same with almonds for extra E. Enjoy your E!

This lowfat meal is a breeze to throw together. Even with preparing the chicken breasts yourself, this meal takes less than 15 minutes to get on the table! Notice that the name is "Hot & Spicy"? The name is accurate. It is hot!

HOT & SPICY CHICKEN **10**
Makes 4 servings

3 1/4 cups boiling water
3 cups INSTANT BROWN RICE *(Uncle Ben's)*

2 tsp. sunflower oil
2 boneless chicken breast halves, thinly sliced
2 garlic cloves, minced
1 medium onion, chopped
2 celery ribs, sliced
1 large green bell pepper, chopped (use the seeds)
4 oz fresh mushrooms, sliced
2 medium tomatoes, chopped

SAUCE:
3/4 cup cold water
1 TB soy sauce
1 pkg. Kung Pao Chicken, Seasoning Mix *(S&B)*

Simmer rice, covered, in the boiling water for 10 minutes. (Do not add butter or salt to the water.)

While the rice simmers, sauté chicken in oil in a large skillet until there is no pink showing. Add remaining vegetables, and simmer for just a couple minutes.

While this is simmering, stir together the sauce mixture. (I like to use a 2 cup measuring cup.) Stir the sauce into the simmering chicken & veggies. Heat till bubbly.

Serve this mixture on top of the brown rice. Enjoy!

This dish is great for those who like hot & spicy food, but it may be too hot for those who like more bland food. For a less spicy sauce, use only part of the Kung Pao packet.

NOTE: You might want to double this recipe to have some left over to freeze in individual packages. Now, you will have your own frozen dinners to pop in the microwave!

HOT & SPICY CHICKEN

Per Serving:

Calories: 445   *Sodium: 805 mg*

Fat: 6.5 g   *Fiber: 7 g*

TIDBIT...

VITAMINS LINKED TO
HEART DISEASE PREVENTION

A recent study looked at people with blockages in the blood vessels of the heart, brain and legs. This study, published in *Circulation*, the American Heart Association Journal, showed that vitamins **B-6** and **folic acid** play a role in the prevention of heart disease and strokes.

GOOD SOURCES OF B-6
& FOLIC ACID

All Legumes such as:

Pinto beans	Soybeans
Black beans	Blackeye peas
Lentils	Lima beans
Garbanzo beans	Red beans

Whole wheat	Wheat germ
Brown rice	Whole corn meal

Green, leafy vegetables

I like this dish because I dirty only one pot! (Who likes to wash dishes?) This takes less than 15 minutes to fix, it is packed with nutrients; complex carbohydrates, vitamins, minerals, fiber, etc. - AND, it is very low in fat.

EGGPLANT WITH TURKEY   **11**
Makes 8 servings

1 tsp. sunflower oil

1 medium onion, chopped

2 garlic cloves, minced

1 medium green bell pepper, chopped (use the seeds)

1 can (15 oz) Italian Tomato Sauce (*Hunt's*)

**2 cans (14 1/2 oz each) chicken broth
    (*Swanson, 1/3 Less Sodium*)**

1 pound eggplant, diced but not peeled

**1 pound thinly sliced, cooked turkey or chicken torn
    into bits (Deli meat is great to use.)**

2 1/2 cups INSTANT BROWN RICE (*Uncle Ben's*)

2 TB Italian Seasoning

Pepper to taste

Sauté onion & garlic in hot oil. Add remaining ingredients. Heat to boiling, then turn to lowest heat, cover and simmer for 10 minutes. That's all!

Serve with whole wheat bread, if you'd like.

If you want a low salt meal, use a "no salt" tomato sauce, and use a bit more Italian seasoning.

This truly is a yummy meal, and there should be enough left over to heat up for lunch tomorrow. Enjoy!

FOOD FOR THOUGHT
Throw the bathrooms scales away! Let's not play mental games with ourselves. With those darned scales, we get excited when we lose five pounds, even though it may be just water. Then we get depressed when we gain five pounds, even though it may be all muscle acquired through our new exercise program.

EGGPLANT WITH TURKEY

Per Serving:

Calories: 220   *Sodium: 1170 mg*

Fat: 2.5 g   *Fiber: 3.4 g*

TIDBIT...

FIBER... *MOTHER NATURE'S HELPER*

Fiber acts like a speeding car when it comes to getting food particles through the digestive tract quickly. This helps prevent constipation, and it quickly removes toxins from the intestines.

Fiber also helps clear cholesterol from the blood, which reduces the risk of stroke and heart disease.

HOW MUCH FIBER?

Health professionals recommend 25 to 30 grams of fiber daily. Personally, I think we should get more.

WHERE DO WE GET FIBER?

Only plant food has fiber. Animal food has no fiber at all. This includes beef, pork, chicken, turkey, fish, eggs, cheese, milk, etc.

In addition, many of the plant foods we eat have been highly processed and do not contain much fiber. Examples: pretzels, bagels, flour tortillas, bread, rolls, biscuits, crackers, etc.

For more about FIBER, see page 70.

This recipe takes less than 15 minutes to get to the table and tastes fantastic!

SIMPLY SOUTHWEST   **12**
Makes 4 large servings

1 can (14 1/2 oz) chicken broth
    (*Swanson, 1/3 Less Sodium*)
2 1/4 cups INSTANT BROWN RICE (*Uncle Ben's*)

2 tsp. sunflower oil
1 medium onion, chopped
2 garlic cloves, minced

2 cups diced cooked turkey (*Louis Rich*)
2 cups (2 small) thinly sliced zucchini
1 medium red bell pepper, chopped (use the seeds)
1 tsp. ground cumin
1/2 cup picante sauce (*Pace*)

Whole wheat bread (*optional, but recommended*)

Bring broth to boil; add rice. Cover and simmer on lowest heat 8 to 10 minutes. While it simmers, sauté onion & garlic in the oil. Add remaining ingredients to the onion/garlic mixture, and cook for just a very few minutes - just till the vegetables are tender-crisp. Serve the turkey mixture on top of the rice. (I may have a slice of Earth Grain whole wheat bread with this meal.)

This dish can be made extra hot & spicy by the kind of picante sauce you use. Use 'hot' picante sauce for an extra hot dish, or use 'mild' sauce for just a bit of spicy flavor.

Green bell pepper can be substituted for red, but the red pepper makes this a beautiful dish, plus it 'ups' the beta carotene tremendously.

Also, you can use leftover cooked chicken or turkey. I like to bake a small turkey just to have meat available for dishes like this.

For variety, experiment with different vegetables the next time you make this dish. A suggestion; try thin carrot slices and bite size pieces of cauliflower. Be creative.

This dish is very low in fat - and it tastes great! Enjoy.

SIMPLY SOUTHWEST

Per Serving (without bread):

Calories: 365   *Sodium: 545 mg*

Fat: 7 g   *Fiber: 4.3 g*

TIDBIT...

FIBER....cont.

FIBER CAN HELP US LOSE WEIGHT

A SECRET to losing weight and maintaining weight loss is FIBER. When we eat a lot of high-fiber foods, we naturally maintain a healthy weight. This is a very simple truth - yet, in our American society, with so much highly processed food, getting a lot of fiber can be difficult.

If we eat plenty of fresh fruits and vegetables along with <u>whole</u> grains and legumes EVERYDAY, we will get plenty of fiber - not only for weight maintenance, but for good health.

DRINK LOTS 'A WATER

It is **very** important to drink plenty of water when eating more fiber. Six to eight cups a day is recommended.

For a list of common foods and their fiber content, see page 72.

Want a fun meal that's super quick to fix and very nutritious - plus low in fat? Then this one's for you.

VEGGIE SPUD 13
Makes 1 serving

1 medium BAKING POTATO

1 tsp. sunflower oil
1 small garlic clove, minced
2 green onions (use entire onion)
1 cup frozen vegetables (California Style)

1/4 cup shredded, low moisture, part skim mozzarella cheese

Put potato in microwave to cook. (Of course, scrub and puncture it.) Sauté veggies in oil just until they're tender-crisp. After the potato is cooked, cut in half and mash a bit with a fork. Pour veggies over the potato, and top with shredded cheese.

If you want your potato to have more moisture, just add a little plain nonfat yogurt when you mash it. This takes the place of high-fat sour cream.

This is one of the meals I like to throw together when I'm in a hurry. I nearly always have these ingredients on hand for those times when I haven't planned ahead.

If you want more servings, just increase everything as needed.

FOOD FOR THOUGHT

When humans are given complete freedom of choice, we tend to make choices based solely on "immediate" pleasures without any thought for the consequences of tomorrow. In the writings of W.C. Fields, he once described this human weakness in this way, "Once during the prohibition, I was forced to live for days on nothing but food and water."

VEGGIE SPUD

Per Serving:

Calories: 460	*Sodium: 250 mg*
Fat: 5 g	*Fiber: 10 g*

TIDBIT...

SUPER SOURCES OF FIBER

ITEM	SERVING	FIBER
BREAD/CEREAL/CRACKERS		
Corn tortilla	1 small	1g
Bread, Honey Wheat Berry	1 slice	2g
Rye Crackers (RYVITA)	2 slices	3g
Raisin Bran	1 cup	8g
LEGUMES		
Black Beans	1/2 cup	5g
Pinto Beans	1/2 cup	6g
Great Northern Beans	1/2 cup	7g
GRAINS		
Brown Rice	1/2 cup	2g
Bulgur	1/2 cup	2g
Whole Wheat Pasta	1/2 cup	6g
FRUITS		
VEGETABLES		
Apple w/o skin	1 small	2g
Apple w/ skin	1 small	3g
Banana	1 small	2g
Orange	1 small	2g
Pear w/o skin	1/2 lg	2g
Pear w/ skin	1/2 lg	3g
Broccoli	1/2 cup	2g
Carrots	1/2 cup	2g
Corn	1/2 cup	3g
Green Peas	1/2 cup	3g
Potato w/ skin	1 small	2g

When we include legumes and whole grains in our daily diets,
we can easily get the 25 to 30 grams of fiber that is recommended daily.

Many people like taboli (tabbouleh) but the high fat content keeps many of us away from it. The following version is packed with energy and is low in fat while it retains all the scrumptious flavor of the high fat variety.

TABOLI SALAD 14
Makes 15, one cup servings

9 cups very hot tap water
3 cups (1 pound) TABOLI WHEAT (bulgur)

5 large tomatoes
2 bunches green onions (use entire onion)
1 bunch fresh parsley

DRESSING:
1/3 cup sunflower oil
1/3 cup lemon juice *(fresh, or frozen Minute Maid)*
3 garlic cloves, minced
1 tsp. salt

Soak wheat in the hot water for 15 minutes. While it's soaking, chop the tomatoes, onions, and parsley. (Be sure to use a big bowl, because this makes a lot!) Mix the dressing ingredients in a glass measuring cup. After the wheat has soaked, drain it well, then mix all ingredients together in the big bowl. If you want a tangier taste, add more lemon juice.

The energy in this meal comes from the taboli wheat (bulgur). Bulgur is very similar in energy to other whole grains, only with a little different flavor. Some people really get "hooked" on this dish. See what you think. (This is a vegetarian dish. To get vitamin B12, just add some animal food; nonfat yogurt, lowfat cottage cheese, or low moisture, part skim mozzarella cheese.)

If you want to use a food processor to chop your veggies, go right ahead. Even though I have one, I like to chop food in my hands.

I know this recipe makes a lot of taboli salad, but this dish gets better (the flavors mix) when it sets in the refrigerator. Also, it is great to have leftovers to take to work. Enjoy!

TABOLI SALAD

Per Serving:

Calories: 155   *Sodium: 170 mg*

Fat: 6.8 g   *Fiber: 4.6 g*

TIDBIT...

CALCIUM ... WHY ARE WE LOSING IT?

We are met with a barrage of advertising telling us to drink or eat certain foods, to take certain mineral combinations, to do certain exercises - all to help us have strong bones. Yet, our hospitals and nursing homes have many people with porous, broken bones. WHY? What are we doing, or not doing, that causes so many of us to be at risk for porous bones?

ANIMAL PROTEIN

I believe that our over-consumption of animal protein is the single biggest reason we have so much problem with porous bones.

You see, when we eat animal protein, we create a low pH in our bodies. A low pH means we have an acid system. (A high pH would be an alkaline system.) For our bodies to function properly, something must occur to neutralize this acid condition that we have created by eating animal protein. So, what happens? Calcium is a neutralizer, and it is pulled from our bones to increase the alkalinity and create a neutral pH.

The more animal protein we eat, the more calcium is pulled from our bones.

Where do we get animal protein? See page 76 for more information.

This definitely is a "stay with you" meal. It's quick too - only 15 minutes, and it's on the table!

QUICK BARLEY & TUNA PILAF **15**
Makes 5 servings

1/2 cup chopped onion
2 garlic cloves, minced
2 cans (14 1/2 oz each) chicken broth
      (Swanson, 1/3 Less Sodium)
1 box (11 oz) QUICK BARLEY *(Quaker)*
2 cups FROZEN PEAS
1 medium red bell pepper, chopped (use the seeds)
1 can (6 1/2 oz) water pack tuna, drained
Pepper to taste

In a large skillet, heat a small amount of chicken broth (about 1/4 cup). Sauté onion & garlic in the broth. Add remaining broth & heat to boiling. Add remaining ingredients; reduce heat, cover & simmer for 10 minutes. That's it!!

This makes a very pretty meal because of the red pepper and the green peas. I would serve whole wheat bread with this meal, as well as carrot sticks.

If you feel that you must have more salt, add just a little. The chicken broth and the tuna both contain plenty of sodium. For those of you who need a very low sodium meal, use salt free tuna.

This makes a lot of pilaf, which is great to have for leftovers. Take some to work with you for lunch, or have the leftovers later.

FOOD FOR THOUGHT
We must stay informed. We must know what the food industry is going to be serving us at our next meal. To help choose foods free of harmful additives and preservatives, use *The Food Storage Bible*. See page 128.

QUICK BARLEY & TUNA PILAF

Per Serving:

Calories: 305	*Sodium: 575 mg*
Fat: 1.8 g	*Fiber: 8.7 g*

TIDBIT...

ANIMAL PROTEIN

Where do we get animal protein? Here is a short list:

MILK	Eggs
Cheese	Beef
Yogurt	Chicken
Cottage cheese	Turkey
Buttermilk	Fish

I can hear you say, "But we're told to drink milk to get the calcium we need for strong bones." It is true that milk and most dairy products are good sources of calcium, but because these are animal foods, they create an acid condition in our bodies, thus causing a depletion of calcium from our bones and teeth.

To look at calcium from another angle, see page 78.

When the weather is cold, our thoughts automatically turn to soups and stews, but crock pot soups and stews are great anytime of the year. Crock pot meals are so easy to throw together in a matter of minutes and they'll be waiting on us in the evening. This meal takes only 7 minutes to toss in the pot before we leave for work in the morning. And this meal is very low in fat and high in energy.

ITALIAN SOUP   **16**
Makes 15, one cup servings

6 medium carrots*
1 large onion
2 garlic cloves
3 celery ribs
3 cans (16 oz each) tomatoes *(Del Monte Italian Stewed)*
5 cups hot water
1 TB Italian Seasoning
Pepper to taste

2 cups INSTANT BROWN RICE

Low moisture, part skim mozzarella cheese (optional)

Scrub the carrots, leave whole and put in bottom of crock pot - put largest carrots on the very bottom. Slice the onion as you would an apple, cut celery in bite-size pieces; add the canned tomatoes, hot water, seasoning and pepper. Let cook on low heat 10-12 hours.

As soon as you get home, turn the heat to high, and add the brown rice. Cover and cook for 15 minutes. Do not lift the lid before 15 minutes.

This is a vegetarian meal with no vitamin B12. Every meal doesn't have to have B12, but if you want, serve thin slices of mozzarella cheese on whole grain crackers to get B12 in this meal.

*When carrots are left whole, they have a much better flavor (and it saves time to leave them whole).

ITALIAN SOUP

Per Serving (without cheese):

Calories: 90	*Sodium: 410 mg*
Fat: .5 g	*Fiber: 3.7 g*

TIDBIT...

FARMER JONES & HIS ACID FIELD

Let's look at this calcium issue from another perspective. When a farmer plants wheat on his farm year after year, his field will become very acid with a low pH. As a result, his field will not produce good wheat. What does he do to make it more alkaline and increase the pH? He adds lime. What is lime? It is calcium.

The correlation between these two examples, the farmer and his acid field and our bodies becoming acid because of too much animal protein, is that an acid condition was created, and calcium was the neutralizer. All the farmer has to do is spread some lime on his field, and his problem is taken care of. It's not so simple for us.

We have created a very risky condition that takes a lot of effort on our parts to correct. If we're big meat & cheese eaters and milk drinkers, it won't be easy for us to change.

For information on what we can do, see page 80.

What do you do with leftover turkey? Why not make chili with it?

A few years ago, we thought that chili should be made only with ground beef or ground pork. Lately we have discovered that chili tastes pretty good made with ground turkey. In fact, many people can't tell the difference in these chilies.

Have you tried chili made with cooked turkey? Talk about quick & easy! This goes together in a very few minutes. The recipe below takes about 10 minutes. This is my kind of meal!!

SPEEDY CHILI **17**
Makes 6, one cup servings

1 tsp. sunflower oil
1 cup chopped onion
1 minced garlic clove

1 cup cooked turkey, cut in small pieces
2 cans (16 oz each) CHILI HOT BEANS *(Bush's)*
1 can (14 1/2 oz) tomatoes
1/2 package Chili Seasoning Mix *(Williams)*

Sauté onion and garlic in the oil. Add remaining ingredients, and heat till bubbly. That's all!!

EAT WITH THIS:
Whole grain crackers, carrot sticks & cauliflower florets.

Now if you're watching your sodium intake, you will want to purchase "No Salt" tomatoes. You will also want to rinse the chili beans. Most all chili seasoning mixes are loaded with salt, but Williams isn't. It is salt free.

Since this recipe makes only 6 cups, I suggest doubling or tripling the recipe. This freezes well, thus making it very handy to pop in the microwave after a busy day. Also, it is convenient to freeze individual servings to take to work with you.

Many chilies are quite high in fat. Rest assured, this one is extremely low. When your friends ask how you can eat chili and not gain weight, just sorta smile and walk on! (On second thought, tell them about *15 MINUTE STORAGE MEALS!*)

SPEEDY CHILI

Per Serving:

Calories: 195	*Sodium: 680 mg*
Fat: 2.7 g	*Fiber: 8 g*

TIDBIT...

HELP IS JUST AROUND THE CORNER

So, how do we balance our acid system and keep the calcium in our bones and teeth? We reduce the animal food we eat, and we increase quality plant foods.

I can hear your question; "Is there enough calcium in plant foods to give us what we need?" Many plant foods are good sources of *absorbable* calcium, and they do not create an acid condition which depletes calcium. Here are some plant foods to eat for calcium:

Dried figs	Legumes (beans, peas, & lentils)
Tofu	Papaya
Broccoli	Collards
Oranges	Asparagus
Cabbage	Turnip greens
Mustard greens	Raisins
Prunes	Mulberries
Mango	Beet greens
Kale	Chard
Cabbage	Okra
Dandelion greens	Tempeh
Miso	Soybeans

As we can see, there is a good variety of plant foods from which we can choose. (Notice how many are _dark_ in color.) Experiment and try them all. Enjoy!

This recipe doesn't sound very original, but it is. It is very low in fat. Most all Tuna Noodle Casserole recipes I know about call for sour cream. Here, we use nonfat yogurt instead of sour cream. This is a one-dish meal. (We dirty two pans to fix it, but everything we need for a complete meal is combined into one dish.) This casserole takes less than 15 minutes to get to the table!

TUNA NOODLE CASSEROLE   18
Makes 5 large servings

4 cups boiling water
3 cups WHOLE WHEAT NOODLES

1 medium onion, chopped
1 tsp. sunflower oil
1 cup plain nonfat yogurt
2 tsp. Worcestershire Sauce
1 can (6 1/2 oz) water packed tuna*
3 cups frozen mixed vegetables**
Pepper to taste

Cook noodles in boiling water for 8 minutes. While they're cooking, brown the onion in oil. Add the remaining ingredients and cook until hot - about 5 minutes. Drain the noodles, then combine everything into one dish. Serve with whole wheat bread.

This is an excellent one-dish, high energy casserole that we really enjoy. See what you think!

*Mackerel or salmon can be substituted for the tuna. Use the bones for more calcium.

**Choose mixed vegetables your family enjoys such as cauliflower, carrots, and green beans. You may certainly use fresh veggies instead of frozen.

FOOD FOR THOUGHT
Without fiber in our foods, it's difficult to know when we're full. We just keep right on eating.

TUNA NOODLE CASSEROLE

Per Serving:

Calories: 220   Sodium: 225 mg

Fat: 2.25 g   Fiber: 6.3 g

TIDBIT...

COKES & TEETH

We know that more than our bones are made of calcium. Our teeth are, too. Scientists agree that decalcification, or the loss of calcium, is the first step in the breakdown of tooth enamel.

So, how do our teeth lose calcium? We know about the loss of calcium due to the consumption of animal protein, but there's more. How about colas?

A study was done using the following soft drinks: Coca-Cola, Pepsi, RC, Dr. Pepper, Crystal Pepsi, Diet Coke, Diet Pepsi, Diet Rite (also called Diet RC), and Diet Dr. Pepper. This study showed the effects of each of these drinks on tooth enamel.*

Damage was evident even 1 HOUR after drinking Coca-Cola!

To drink colas, or not to drink colas - the choice is ours.

For further information, see page 84.
*The Angle Orthodontist, Vol. 66, #6, 1996. pg 449-456

Pasta salads are great anytime, but a cold pasta salad is particularly inviting in summertime. This very tasty salad takes less than 15 minutes to get to the table and there is only one pan to wash!

MINESTRONE SALAD   **19**
Makes 8, one cup servings

3 cups boiling water
2 cups WHOLE WHEAT PASTA

2 cans (15 oz each) BLACK BEANS, rinsed (*Ranch Style*)
2 cans (14 oz each) Italian stewed tomatoes
1 bunch green onions, chopped (use entire onion)
1 garlic clove, minced
Pepper to taste

Shredded, low moisture, part skim mozzarella (optional)

Cook pasta in boiling water for 10 minutes. (I like to use whole wheat macaroni.) While it is cooking, prepare remaining ingredients and put in a serving bowl. Add the drained pasta & stir. That's all! Top with a small amount of shredded mozzarella if you want.

This dish is a complete protein without the cheese. The black beans, a legume, and the pasta, a grain, make this a complete protein - however, it has no vitamin B12. The cheese provides B12 and more flavor - and some fat.

This is a great dish to fix when you get home in the evening, or fix it early in the morning so it will be ready in the evening when you walk in the house. (This salad is good hot or cold.) Many of us are busy with childrens' ball games, dance lessons, etc. in the evenings, and this quick-to-fix meal will be a godsend for those busy days. Do give this a try.

FOOD FOR THOUGHT
The diet industry's favorite slogan: "We never cure them. We never kill them. But they just keep coming back and spending more and more money."

MINESTRONE SALAD

Per Serving (without cheese):

Calories: 215 *Sodium: 720 mg*

Fat: .5 g *Fiber: 10 g*

TIDBIT...

COKES & BONES

Doesn't it make sense that if colas decalcify teeth, they do the same to bones? Absolutely! The phosphoric acid in soft drinks creates an acid condition, or low pH. What occurs to increase the alkalinity and create a neutral pH? Calcium is pulled from the bones.

If you are a heavy consumer of soft drinks and phosphoric acid, this certainly gives you something to think about. Phosphoric acid is found in more places than just soft drinks. Look at some of your processed foods and see where you find it.

It's no wonder we have porous bones! Because of our diet, we have created a very acid body condition which must be neutralized by drawing calcium from our bones and teeth.

To solve this problem, we must make changes in our diet. Begin by eating more fresh fruits and vegetables and less animal foods. Also, decrease the use of soft drinks.

The choice is ours.

Did you know that Americans consume more than 10 billion bowls of soup each year? In the month of January, we buy 57 million gallons of soup. This averages 100 cans of condensed soup every second of every day in January!

Soup is so convenient to pack in a lunch pail or take to the office. Soup can come in a can, a box, a microwaveable cup, a cellophane bag, and it even comes frozen. Unfortunately sodium and fat are high in many soups. However, we can make our own. This potato soup is a favorite with my family and takes only 15 minutes to get to the table.

POTATO SOUP   20
Makes 9, one cup servings

1 tsp. sunflower oil
1 medium onion, chopped
3 garlic cloves, minced
2 celery ribs, sliced
2 cans (14 1/2 oz each) chicken broth
     (*Swanson, 1/3 Less Sodium*)
3 medium POTATOES, cut in *small* pieces

2 cups skim milk*
1 TB dried parsley flakes (or 1/4 cup fresh)
Pepper to taste

Sauté onion in oil; add ingredients through potatoes and heat to boiling. Simmer 10 minutes on medium-high heat, uncovered. Add remaining ingredients and stir. Serve in soup bowls or mugs.

Serve with whole wheat crackers or whole wheat pretzels and raw veggies such as carrot sticks, green pepper slices, cauliflower, etc.

* If you have a problem with milk, use lowfat Acidophilus or soy milk.

An old Yiddish saying: "Troubles are easier to take with soup than without."

An old Spanish proverb: "Of soup and love, the first is best."

POTATO SOUP

Per Serving:

Calories: 120   *Sodium: 290 mg*

Fat: .6 g   *Fiber: 1.7 g*

TIDBIT...

5 OR MORE A DAY

"Eat 5 or more servings a day of a variety of fruits & vegetables all year round". This is a recommendation from scientists who tell us that by eating "5 or more a day", overall cancer incidence rates could decline by as much as 20%!!!

SERVINGS:

What constitutes a serving? This can be confusing, so let's look at serving sizes.

FOOD	AMOUNT	EXAMPLE
Fresh fruit:	1 small fruit	1 small orange, 1 small banana
Fresh fruit:	1/2 cup cut-up	any fruit
Fresh vegetables:	1/2 cup raw	any vegetable lightly steamed
Fresh vegetables:	1 cup leafy greens	leaf lettuce, spinach, kale, romaine, etc.
Beans or peas:	1/2 cup cooked	any legume (kidney, pinto, lentil, etc.)
Dried fruit:	1/4 cup	any fruit
Juice:	6 ounces	any fruit or vegetable

KEEP THEM VISIBLE

'Out of sight is out of mind'. Make fresh fruits & vegetables more visible at home - and at work. Keep a bowl of fruit on the table for a quick snack.

Many times people have asked me how to cook a pot of beans if ham isn't used for flavoring. (The reason I choose not to use cured ham is that it contains cancer-causing nitrites and is high in fat.)

My family just loves the flavor and zip of these beans. If you want to use some meat (animal flesh) just add a couple of skinned chicken breasts or a few skinned thighs.

PEPPY PINTOS   21
Makes 11, one cup servings

3 1/2 cups dried PINTO BEANS
7 cups hot water
1 medium onion, chopped
1 can (7 oz) chopped green chilies
4 garlic cloves, minced
1 1/2 TB chili powder
1 tsp. salt (optional)

Wash pintos thoroughly (looking for small stones). Add all ingredients to a crock pot. Stir and cook on low heat 12 hours or longer.

EAT WITH THIS:
     Corn bread
     Carrot sticks
     Cauliflower florets

If you don't want to take the time to make corn bread, just eat whole grain crackers or Guiltless Gourmet Tortilla Chips.

It's a real treat to walk in the house on a cold blustery evening after work and smell a pot of beans ready to eat. I hope you like this version of cooked pintos as much as we do.

FOOD FOR THOUGHT
We say we don't have the energy to exercise. That's understandable. It is difficult to have energy when we don't eat the energy foods.

PEPPY PINTOS

Per Serving (includes salt):

Calories: 70   *Sodium: 310 mg*

Fat: .28 g   *Fiber: 3.5 g*

TIDBIT...

WHAT ARE
3 SIMPLE CHANGES
AMERICANS CAN MAKE
FOR BETTER HEALTH?

(1) Walk more

(2) Eat more fresh fruits and vegetables

(3) Laugh more

As it says in the Bible,
"A merry heart doeth good like a medicine."
Proverbs 17:22

So many people love this dish! It's quick to fix, it's very tasty, very low in fat, and it's filled with energy.

LAREDO POTATO 22
Makes 1 serving

1 medium POTATO
1/4 cup CHILI HOT BEANS *(Bush's)*
1/2 tomato, chopped
2 TB chopped green onion
1/2 oz shredded, low moisture, part skim
mozzarella cheese

2 TB Salsa *(Pace)*

Bake potato in microwave 4 minutes - or till done; split and mash a bit. Top with the beans. Heat in microwave. Top with tomato, onion, and cheese. Now add salsa for great Mexican flavor.

EAT WITH THIS:
1 small carrot
1/2 medium green pepper

This is soooooooo quick and easy! And it's packed with gobs of energy and is very lowfat. Keep the ingredients on hand, and you'll always have a tasty meal available.

I strongly recommend low moisture, part skim mozzarella cheese as it is lower in fat, cholesterol and sodium than other natural cheeses.

FOOD FOR THOUGHT
God gave us two ends. One to sit on and one to think with. Health depends upon which one we use most. Heads we win. Tails we lose.

LAREDO POTATO

Per Serving:

Calories: 320   Sodium: 560 mg

Fat: 3 g   Fiber: 9.5 g

TIDBIT...

FRESH TOMATOES...
Are they always a good choice?

Are fresh tomatoes always a good choice? No, not always. And the answer depends upon the tomato, or more specifically, where it was raised.

What does place of origin have to do with anything? Even though the United States uses *many* pesticides, we outlaw some that are particularly dangerous, BUT, we continue to manufacture these pesticides and sell to countries which are allowed to use them. Then what do we do? We import foods that have been treated with the banned pesticides!

The Roma tomato is one of the most prevalent fresh items in our produce section that is raised outside the U.S.. Some Romas are from the States, but most are from Mexico.

If you aren't sure, just ask the produce person where the fresh produce is raised.

One of the reasons we hardly ever see overweight, native, Oriental people is because of the way they eat. If we eat meals like this one on a regular basis, people will say the same about us!

ORIENTAL BEEF & VEGETABLE STIR-FRY   23
Makes 6 servings

2 1/4 cups boiling water
2 cups INSTANT BROWN RICE *(Uncle Ben's)*

1 pound *lean* **beef (loins are best)**
1 tsp. sunflower oil
2 cups broccoli florets
2 cups chunked, fresh mushrooms
1 medium red bell pepper, chopped (use the seeds)

1 TB cornstarch
1 TB soy sauce
3/4 cup cold water

Add rice to the boiling water; cover and simmer on lowest heat for 10 minutes. While the rice cooks, trim all fat from meat & slice thinly. In a large skillet, brown meat in hot oil; add vegetables and stir.

Mix cornstarch, soy sauce and water; add to skillet, stir and cover. Reduce heat and cook until sauce thickens - maybe one minute. Serve over the rice.

You may certainly use regular brown rice. In fact, I like the flavor and texture of regular brown rice better than quick cooking. It just takes longer to cook. When you're not in a hurry, use the regular rice - brown, that is - and see what you think.

This is a beautiful, nutritious, lowfat and high energy meal. It is one of my favorite meals to serve to dinner guests.

FOOD FOR THOUGHT
95% of all diets fail - which makes dieters failures. Kinda' hard to have a good, positive attitude as a failure!

ORIENTAL BEEF & VEGETABLE STIR-FRY

Per Serving:

Calories: 315   *Sodium: 295 mg*

Fat: 9 g   *Fiber: 3.3 g*

TIDBIT...

BURNING CALORIES

Do you want to burn some extra calories? To see how many calories are burned *per minute* per activity, look below:

ACTIVITY	WEIGHT IN POUNDS			
	(105-115)	(127-137)	(160-170)	(182-192)
Heavy snow shoveling	13.8	15.7	18.5	20.4
Cross country skiing, 9mph	13.4	15.7	17.6	19.3
Stationary bicycling, 20mph	11.7	13.3	15.6	17.2
Fullcourt basketball	9.8	11.2	13.2	14.5
Jogging, 5 mph	8.6	9.8	11.5	12.7
Downhill skiing	7.8	10.4	12.3	13.3
Stair climbing	5.9	6.7	7.9	8.8
Aerobic dancing	5.8	6.6	7.2	8.6
Stationary bicycling, 10 mph	5.5	6.3	7.4	8.2
Bicycling, 10mph	5.4	6.2	7.3	7.9
Walking, 4 mph	4.5	5.2	6.1	6.8
Swimming, 20 yd/min	3.9	4.5	5.3	6.8
Golf with handcart	3.3	3.8	4.4	4.9
Walking, 2 mph	2.4	2.8	3.3	3.6

Adapted from Your Health, 1990 Prentice Hall

If we eat an extra 200 calories, it's easy to see how much we need to do to work it off. We either work it off, or it becomes a part of us!

I get many requests for recipes that do not contain meat, yet still provide complete protein. This recipe is one of my favorites. It is a very high energy meal, very lowfat, high in fiber, and it's quick to fix.

VEGETARIAN CHILI   24

Makes 8, one cup servings

1 tsp. sunflower oil
1/2 cup chopped onion
2 garlic cloves, minced
2 cups INSTANT BROWN RICE *(Uncle Ben's)*
2 cans (14 1/2 oz each) tomatoes
2 cans (16 oz each) CHILI HOT BEANS *(Bush's)*
1/2 package chili seasoning mix *(Williams)*

Sauté onion & garlic in oil; add remaining ingredients. Heat to boiling, then reduce heat. Cover & simmer for 10 minutes. (If you want a thinner chili, just add some water. If you like a spicier chili, add more seasoning mix.)

EAT WITH THIS:
   WHOLE GRAIN CRACKERS or
   WHOLE GRAIN CORN BREAD
   Carrot sticks
   Raw cauliflower, or cabbage or broccoli

(Use whatever raw veggies your family likes.) Enjoy!

FOOD FOR THOUGHT

75% of the products on our grocery shelves are absolutely worthless to us. (Maybe more in some stores!) How should we shop? We should find the "Fabulous 30" foods - put them in our cart, then spend the rest of our time deciding which fruits and vegetables look the best, and put them in our cart. Now, what should we do? Go home and enjoy eating and eating - without guilt for a change!

VEGETARIAN CHILI

Per Serving:

Calories: 225   Sodium: 595 mg

Fat: 2.2 g   Fiber: 7 g

TIDBIT...

WHAT DO MILK LABELS TELL US?

Is 2% milk lowfat? Hardly! Many people think when they drink 2%, they're drinking lowfat. Not so!! The 2% on milk labels means that the *weight* of the fat in the milk is 2% - not the percentage of calories. Two percent milk is actually 38% fat! This is a far cry from being lowfat!

What are milk labels telling us? A one cup serving has:

MILK	LISTING	GRAMS OF FAT	CALORIES
Skim	Fat-free or Nonfat	0	80
1/2 %	Lowfat	1	90
1 %	Light	2.5	100
2%	Reduced-fat	5	120
Homogenized*	Whole	8	150

* 'Homogenized' is truly a misnomer as all milk sold in grocery stores in homogenized.

SUGGESTION: If you're wanting to go to a lower percentage milkfat but just can't 'stomach' the skim or 1%, make the change gradually. Mix a portion of what you're presently using with a portion of skim milk. Gradually decrease the portion of higher fat milk while increasing the lower fat. You'll get there, and you'll be healthier for it!

Many people enjoy muffins. They are a grab-and-run food, and they make great snacks. They can also be health hazards because many 'store muffins' are made with nutrient deficient flour, and they're high in fat and sugar. These applesauce muffins are healthful. They're made with whole wheat flour and no sugar.

APPLESAUCE MUFFINS 25
Makes 36 mini muffins

2 cups WHOLE WHEAT FLOUR
(or whole wheat pastry flour)
1 TB baking powder *(Rumford)*
1 tsp. baking soda
1/2 tsp. nutmeg
1/2 tsp. cinnamon
1 cup raisins
1/2 cup chopped pecans

1 1/2 cups unsweetened applesauce
1 egg

Heat oven to 375°.

Put all dry ingredients in a large bowl, making sure there are no lumps in the baking soda, and stir until the ingredients are well mixed. Make a 'well' in the center of the mixture; add applesauce and egg. Stir applesauce and egg together until the egg is mixed in, then blend dry ingredients into the applesauce/egg mixture. Stir just until moistened. (By mixing the ingredients this way, you dirty only one bowl!)

Fill lightly greased mini muffin cups 2/3 full. Bake 12-15 minutes.

FOOD FOR THOUGHT

We say it's awfully hard to resist temptation for those rich, fat-filled foods. Yes, I know. Do I ever know!! But I'll guarantee one thing, it's a lot easier to resist them when you're full than when you're on some crazy, calorie-counting diet. Just remember this philosophy - "Never Go Hungry."

APPLESAUCE MUFFINS

Per Serving (1 mini muffin):

Calories: 55   *Sodium: 70 mg*

Fat: 1.4 g   *Fiber: 1.6 g*

TIDBIT...

KIDS -
WHAT ARE YOUR KIDS EATING?

A recent study determined that only 1% of American youth ages 2 to 19 eat healthy diets. This study found that most young people eat high fat and high sugar diets. (This is news??)

Remember that bad eating habits in childhood can lead to disease later in life.

SENIORS -
DID YOU KNOW?

Half of all seniors in the U.S. over the age of 65 have some form of arthritis. There are over 100 different forms of arthritis. Studies show that what we eat has an effect on many forms of this crippling disease.

What a simple meal to fix! Kids love macaroni & cheese, but nearly all boxed brands are made with nutrient deficient, highly processed pasta and contain artificial color. So - make your own in the same length of time it takes to make it from a box. Of course, yours will be a lot more healthful and won't add weight to the waistline!

MACARONI & CHEESE, ITALIAN STYLE — 26
Makes 6, one cup servings

3 cups boiling water
2 cups WHOLE WHEAT MACARONI

1 cup spaghetti sauce *(Healthy Choice)*
2 garlic cloves, minced
2/3 cup fresh parsley (or 2 TB dried)

Low moisture, part skim mozzarella, shredded

Boil macaroni 8 minutes; drain. Put back into saucepan; add spaghetti sauce, garlic and parsley. Heat through and serve. Top each serving with 1/4 cup shredded mozzarella.

EAT WITH THIS:
A variety of veggies raw or steamed, such as:
Broccoli, cauliflower, carrots, green or red pepper.

The whole wheat pasta is packed with energy that kids - moms & dads too - need. Since we use such a small portion of cheese, this dish is lowfat. These ingredients are easy to keep on hand, and you can throw this meal together in nothing flat!

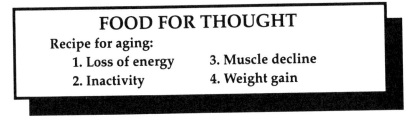

FOOD FOR THOUGHT
Recipe for aging:
1. Loss of energy
2. Inactivity
3. Muscle decline
4. Weight gain

MACARONI & CHEESE ITALIAN STYLE

Per Serving (with cheese):

Calories: 225   *Sodium: 310 mg*

Fat: 5.7 g   *Fiber: 4.6 g*

TIDBIT...

ARE YOU WANTING TO HAVE A BABY?

If you're thinking of having a baby, or someone you care about is wanting to have a baby, serious thought should be given to adequate folic acid intake, according to numerous studies.

Without adequate folic acid, spina bifida can occur during the first month of pregnancy. Spinal bifida occurs when the spine of the fetus fails to close properly.

Where do we get folic acid? *Whole* grain products, legumes (beans, peas, lentils, etc.), dark green leafy vegetables, and wheat germ are highest in folic acid.

The key message is that women wanting to have children should have diets high in folic acid BEFORE becoming pregnant.

This is a great dish to serve at home or take to a luncheon. It will probably be the only one like it there. I can assure you, you will be asked for the recipe!

BROWN RICE WALDORF SALAD 27
Makes 8, one cup servings

1 1/4 cups boiling water
1 cup INSTANT BROWN RICE* *(Uncle Ben's)*

4 medium red apples, diced (do not peel)
2 TB lemon juice *(fresh, or frozen Minute Maid)*
2 TB apple juice concentrate
3 celery ribs, thinly sliced (1 1/2 cups)
1/2 cup chopped pecans
1/2 cup raisins
1 cup plain nonfat yogurt
1/2 tsp. cinnamon
1/4 tsp. nutmeg
1/4 tsp. allspice

Add rice to the boiling water. Turn to lowest heat; cover and simmer for 10 minutes. While it cooks, chop the apples in a serving bowl and add lemon juice to coat the apples. Add the remaining ingredients, including the cooked rice; stir well. Serve immediately or chill for later.

This is a wonderful meal that is filling, lowfat, nutritious, and packed with energy. This is one of our favorite meals, and I love it because I can fix it ahead and have it waiting in the fridge.

*Remember that you can use regular brown rice. In fact, I like the taste and texture of the regular rice, but it does take longer to cook. Use whichever you like.

FOOD FOR THOUGHT
"Real" food does not make us fat. Fats and highly processed foods make us fat.

BROWN RICE WALDORF SALAD

Per Serving:

Calories: 190	*Sodium: 30 mg*
Fat: 5.6 g	*Fiber: 7.5 g*

TIDBIT...

THE SKINNY ON POTATOES

One large baked potato has only .2 gram of fat. Ten potato chips fried in oil, have 8 grams of fat!

POTASSIUM POWER

Which has more potassium, a banana or a potato? A medium banana has 451 mg of potassium while a small potato has 844 mg!

This is a very quick meal that has a unique flavor because of the cabbage and tarragon. I love the flavor, and the dish is so colorful.

TARRAGON TURKEY   **28**
Makes 4 servings

2 cans (14 1/2 oz each) chicken broth
  (*Swanson, 1/3 Less Sodium*)
2 cups INSTANT BROWN RICE (*Uncle Ben's*)

1/2 pound turkey breast, skinned & thinly sliced*
1 tsp. sunflower oil
1 garlic clove, minced
1/2 cup chopped onion
1 tsp. dried tarragon
2 cups shredded cabbage
1 cup chopped celery
1 medium red bell pepper, thinly sliced (use the seeds)

3/4 cup chicken broth (*Swanson, 1/3 Less Sodium*)
1 TB cornstarch

Heat chicken broth to boiling; add brown rice, reduce heat to simmer, cover and cook for 10 minutes.

While rice cooks, brown the turkey on both sides in oil. Add the garlic, onion and tarragon. Stir and add cabbage, celery and red pepper.

Mix broth and cornstarch; add to skillet and stir. Cover and simmer 3-5 minutes. Stir and serve over the rice.

* You may substitute chicken breast for the turkey. The flavor is similar, whichever you use.

This is a high energy, lowfat meal that is full of wonderful veggies packed with nutrients, flavor and color. You may substitute pimentos for the red pepper if you'd like. The red pepper has more nutrients and better flavor, but you may not be able to get them all during the year.

TARRAGON TURKEY

Per Serving:

Calories: 340   Sodium: 760 mg

Fat: 4.7 g   Fiber: 5 g

TIDBIT...

WILL YOU GAIN 10 POUNDS THIS YEAR?

If you eat an extra 100 calories a day - the amount in 2 FAT FREE, SnackWell's Devil's Food Cookie Cakes - you could gain 10 pounds in one year!

AMERICANS DON'T LIKE TO SWEAT!

Even with all we hear & read about the benefits of exercise, still almost 60% of us don't lift much more than our little fingers!

PUMP THAT IRON!

The more muscle we have, the higher our metabolism, and the faster we burn calories. Soooo, pump that iron!!

I cannot describe to you the fantastic flavor this dish has - you just have to experience it for yourself! I call it "Chicken Surprise" because the flavor is unusual, but delicious.

CHICKEN SURPRISE 29
Makes 6 servings

1 can (14 1/2 oz) chicken broth
    (Swanson, 1/3 Less Sodium)
2 cups INSTANT BROWN RICE *(Uncle Ben's)*

1 can (15 oz) BLACK BEANS *(Ranch Style)*
1 cup bite-size, cooked chicken
1/2 cup plain, nonfat yogurt
1/3 cup sliced almonds
2 tsp. soy sauce
1/4 tsp. pepper
1/4 tsp. poultry seasoning

Heat broth to boiling; add rice, cover and simmer on lowest heat for 10 minutes.

While rice is cooking, combine remaining ingredients in a large serving dish. As soon as rice is done, add to serving dish. Mix well and serve immediately. That's all!

If you want to garnish this dish, some slices of tomato or red pepper would be great around the edges, along with some sprigs of parsley. Then sprinkle a few sliced almonds on top.

(You can use Louis Rich Oven Roasted Turkey Breast in place of cooked chicken. Or you can use leftover turkey.)

SUGGESTION: Make a big batch and freeze it for future meals.

Serve some steamed vegetables with this dish; such as broccoli and cauliflower or cabbage.

FOOD FOR THOUGHT

Definitions:

Old people food: Foods that make us fat and age prematurely.

Young people food: Foods that keep us trim, active and healthy.

CHICKEN SURPRISE

Per Serving:

Calories: 260	*Sodium: 590 mg*
Fat: 4.7 g	*Fiber: 5 g*

TIDBIT...

ESTROGEN - FOR MEN!!??

Hey you men out there. Do you think estrogen is only for women? Think again. Studies show that *phytoestrogens (plant estrogens) can be effective in preventing certain cancers* including *prostate and colorectal.* Phytoestrogens can also be effective in preventing *heart disease and kidney disease.* Estrogen has even been shown as a factor in inhibiting *Alzheimer's Disease.*

So men, enjoy plant foods high in estrogen - especially soy foods - right along with women! The next time you have the opportunity to eat a soy burger instead of a hamburger, give it a try. I bet you'll like it!

For foods high in estrogen, see page 106.

All you chocolate lovers out there (which includes me) here's one for you!

CHOCOLATE MUFFINS **30**
Makes 36 mini muffins

1 1/2 cups WHOLE WHEAT FLOUR
or whole wheat pastry flour

6 TB cocoa (or carob)

1 tsp. baking soda

1/2 tsp. baking powder *(Rumford)*

1/4 tsp. salt

1 cup raisins

1/2 cup chopped pecans

2 extra ripe bananas

1 egg

1/3 cup unsweetened applesauce

1/4 cup apple juice concentrate

Turn oven to 350°. In a large bowl, stir together flour, cocoa, soda, baking powder and salt. Add pecans and raisins. (Separate raisins if they're stuck together.)

In another bowl, mash the bananas; fold in egg, applesauce and apple juice concentrate.

Add liquid ingredients to dry ingredients and stir together until moistened.

Fill lightly greased mini muffin cups 2/3 full and bake 12-15 minutes.

These are very high energy, fiber filled muffins. Realize that these are not going to taste like the high fat, sugar filled, nutrient deficient muffins you find in most donut shops. The difference in these muffins and the others is just like the difference in white bread and whole wheat bread.

FOOD FOR THOUGHT
"At 40, I was starting to show my age, but I took my life back in control and now, 10 years later, I'm back to 30!"

CHOCOLATE MUFFINS

Per Serving:

Calories: 55   Sodium: 55 mg

Fat: 1.5 g   Fiber: 1.2 g

TIDBIT...

ESTROGEN IN FOODS

Soy products contain the most estrogen. These include the following:

Tofu	Tempeh
Soy milk	Soybeans
Textured vegetable protein (TVP)	
(Also known as textured soy protein [TSP])	

What is a serving size for these foods?

Tofu	1/2 cup
Tempeh	1/2 cup
Soy milk	1 cup
Soybeans	1/4 cup, cooked
TVP/TSP	1/4 cup, dry

Additional foods that contain estrogen:

Apple	Broccoli
Brussels sprouts	Cabbage
Carrots	Corn*
Flax seed	Garlic
Oats	Pineapple
Peanut	Potato
Rice*	Sesame seed
Whole wheat	Legumes (kidney, pinto, black beans, etc.)

* I feel certain that whole corn products and brown rice contain more estrogen than degerminated corn and white rice. Doesn't it just make sense?

EPILOGUE

The year was 1917 when an educator by the name of Orville Swip made this statement while addressing a high school class in New England:

> "Every person who is not his own master is sure to have somebody or something else for his master sooner or later - usually sooner. Be boss of yourself, of your mind as well as your body, and success is assured."

I hope you enjoy these
quick, healthful meals
as much as my family does.

In Good Health,

Jayne

Jayne

INDEX

THE "FABULOUS 30" FOODS

THE "FABULOUS 30" RECIPES

CONVERTING RECIPES &
USING LONG-COOKING STORAGE FOODS

In many of the recipes in this book, I use instant brown rice or canned beans. If you want to use stored long-cooking rice or dried beans, this is just fine. It's simple to make the change.

With BEANS, just cook your dried beans like you normally do, then add whatever seasoning is required in the recipe. For example, I use canned Chili Hot Beans in some recipes. Instead of using the canned beans from the grocery store, cook your own dried beans then add chili powder, jalapeños, picante sauce, or other Mexican seasoning. The recipe now takes much longer than 15 minutes to prepare, but that's okay.

Bothered with gas? If you have a flatulence problem when eating beans, sprout your beans before cooking. Not only do you eliminate the gas problem, you increase the nutrient content, and you considerably decrease the cooking time. For information on sprouting, see page 119.

Do the same with RICE . Instead of using instant brown rice, cook your own long-cooking stored rice and just replace it for the instant rice in the recipe. Again, this will take longer, but this is fine if time isn't a factor.

Speaking of time - if time is a factor and you want to use long-cooking stored foods, just cook a large batch of rice, beans or whatever, then freeze them. I like to cook a big pot of brown rice, beans, or other grains then freeze 2 cup portions in zip-lock bags or other air-tight containers. Now, I'm prepared for quick meals using my long-cooking grains and beans.

For excellent recipes using stored beans, use *Country Beans* by Rita Bingham. For great recipes using stored wheat, use *Natural Meals In Minutes* also by Rita Bingham, and use *The Amazing Wheat Book* by LeArta Moulton. For more information, see pages 129 and 131.

STOCKING A HEALTHY STORAGE PANTRY

Stocking your pantry with certain staples is vital to good health, as well as for being prepared to fix quick meals - AND for being prepared in case of emergencies. There are many types of emergencies; power failures, floods, tornadoes, earthquakes, hurricanes, financial burdens, and so on. If we always keep certain foods in our pantry, we will be prepared for most any emergency.

STAPLES IN MY KITCHEN

There are certain non-perishable foods and recipe ingredients that I always have on hand. It is wise to store at least one month's supply of non-perishable food for each family member.

Below is a list of products from the grocery store, including some with brand names, that I keep stored at all times. I list brand names because these do NOT contain harmful additives & preservatives.

(I have included perishable foods to show you all the foods I store.)

IN THE PANTRY:
CANNED *
Legumes; (all varieties including;)
    Black beans, Chili Hot Beans, Great Northern Beans *(Bush's)*
Chicken Broth, 1/3 Less Sodium *(Swanson)*
Green chilies
Pasta Sauce, *(Hunt's Ready Tomato Sauces)*
Tomatoes, Italian stewed
Refried Beans; Fat Free *(Rosarita)*
Chicken *(Hormel)*
Mackerel
Salmon
Tuna
BOXED, BAGGED & BOTTLED *
Baking Powder *(Rumford)*
Baking soda
Barley
Biscuit Mix *(Arrowhead Mills)*
Bulgur - Taboli wheat *(Bob's Red Mill)*
Corn Meal *(Arrowhead Mills)*
Corn Bread Mix *(Hodgson Mill)*
Garlic (fresh)

Grape juice (bottled, purple or red)
Legumes (beans for cooking & sprouting)
Milk (powdered)
Muffin Mixes *(Hodgson Mills)*
Oatmeal (old fashioned)
Onions (fresh)
Orange juice (bottled)
Pasta (whole wheat, corn or brown rice)
Peanut butter (natural)
Picante sauce *(Pace)*
Potatoes (fresh)
Raisins (dark)
Rice (instant brown & long cooking brown)
Soy Granules *(Fearn)*
Soy milk (refrigerate after opening) **
Squash (fresh winter)
Sweet potatoes (fresh)
Tofu *(Mori-Nu, Lite)* **
Wheat berries (for cooking & sprouting)
Whole grain cereals *(Grape-Nuts)*
Whole grain crackers *(Health Valley)*
Whole grain corn tortilla chips *(Guiltless Gourmet)*
Whole grain flours *(Bob's Red MIll)*
Whole wheat bread (or Honey Wheat Berry)
Whole wheat flour, stone ground *(Bob's Red Mill)*
Whole wheat pasta *(Pritikin)*

IN THE FRIDGE:
REFRIGERATED
Butter
Cheese (low moisture, part skim mozzarella)
Cheese (soy)
Eggs
Fruits (a variety)
Nuts (a variety)
Seeds (a variety for eating & sprouting, see page 127)
Skim milk
Sunflower oil ***
Vegetables (a wide variety)
Whole grains ****
Whole grain flours ****

FROZEN
Apple juice concentrate
Bananas (for smoothies)
Chicken breasts
Corn
Fish
Peas

ON THE SHELF:
SPICES
Cilantro
Cinnamon
Cumin
Curry
Dill
Ginger
Italian seasonings:
    Basil
    Oregano
    Parsley
    Thyme
Nutmeg
Pepper
Salt, iodized
Turmeric
Vinegar
Worcestershire Sauce

MISCELLANEOUS
Salad Dressing Mix *(Good Season's Fat Free)*
Chili Seasoning Mix *(Williams)*

ON THE TABLE:
FRESH FRUIT
Bananas
Lemons
Oranges
In-season fruits

This may seem like an extensive list, but notice that many of these items you probably already have in your kitchen; example, salt & pepper, eggs, milk, flour, bread, etc. With these items, you will be able to fix many of the recipes in this *15 Minute Storage Meals* cookbook. For some of the recipes you will need to purchase extra ingredients - but very few.

If cooking is a new experience for you, or you don't really like to cook, begin by choosing a recipe that is VERY simple, and one that your family will enjoy. Then keep the ingredients on hand so you will be able to fix it anytime.

After you have one meal perfected, try a new recipe. Look at cooking as an adventure and have fun doing it. If you have children, get them involved. Soon they will enjoy helping make choices in the grocery store and helping you prepare the meal.

Remember that your family's food choices may be different from my family's. You may like different fresh veggies and fruits. That's fine, just keep a variety of fresh foods on hand. Now, HAVE FUN!!

For how much to store, see page 116.

SUGGESTION

I bet there are times when you want something to drink other than water. One of my favorites is what I call, "Jayne's Grape Drink." I fill a glass with ice and water almost to the top. I then add a small amount of purple or red grape juice. Next, I squeeze a lemon or lime wedge into the drink and drop the wedge in the glass. This is VERY tasty as well as nutritious. Give it a try.

* For other name brands, refer to my book, *The Food Storage Bible.* Order number: 1-800-580-1414.

** Products packaged in aseptic packaging don't need to be refrigerated - until after opening.

*** Sunflower oil in the fridge??!! After cooking oil is opened, store it in the refrigerator. Oils become rancid quickly at room temperature. Rancid oil is a great source of immune-damaging free radicals. (Olive oil is an exception. It will not become rancid for at least five years.)

**** Store whole grains in the refrigerator or freezer. Bugs know a good thing when they smell it!

HOW MUCH TO STORE?

It is always wise to have at least a one month supply of food stored in case of emergency. I have figured the amount of food to store for an average adult using ingredients from this cookbook, *15 Minute Storage Meals*. Keep in mind, you will need to purchase the fresh fruits and vegetables required for each recipe.

These are the recipes I have chosen from this book, *15 Minute Storage Meals:*

Albuquerque Special	pg 59
Arroz Con Pollo	pg 47
Barley & Tuna Pilaf	pg 75
Brown Rice Waldorf Salad	pg 99
Chocolate (Carob) Muffins	pg 105
Italian Soup	pg 77
Mexican Quickie	pg 63
Minestrone Salad	pg 83
Peppy Pintos	pg 87
Quick Mexican Salad	pg 55
Spuds & More	pg 53
Vegetarian Chili	pg 93

WHAT TO STORE & HOW MUCH

Below, I list the products required for 60 servings (30 lunches, 30 dinners) of the above recipes, as well as how much of each product is needed for an average adult for one month. (I have also included ingredients for 30 breakfasts.)

CANNED & BOTTLED

☐ 1 (2 lb) jar   Applesauce (no sugar)

☐ 3 (14.5oz) cans   Chicken broth

☐ 1 (15 oz) can   Chicken vegetable soup

☐ 1 (2 qt) jar   Grape juice (purple or red)

☐ 2 (4.5oz) cans   Green chilies

CANNED & BOTTLED, Cont'd
Legumes:

- ❑ 3 (15oz) cans — Black beans
- ❑ 3 (15oz) cans — Chili Hot Beans
- ❑ 1 (15oz) cans — Green Northern beans
- ❑ 1 (1 lb) can — Refried beans
- ❑ 1 (1 lb) jar — Picante sauce
- ❑ 10 (14.5oz) cans — Tomatoes
- ❑ 2 (6.5oz) cans — Tuna (water pack)

BOXED & BAGGED

- ❑ 1 (11oz) box — Barley (quick)
- ❑ 1 (1lb) pkg — Beans, dried (to cook & sprout)
- ❑ 2 (1 lb) loaves — Bread (whole grain)
- ❑ 16 cups — Cereal (hot or cold)
- ❑ 1 (1oz) pkgs — Chili seasoning
- ❑ 4 (7oz) bags — Chips (tortilla)
- ❑ 1/2 cup — Cocoa (or carob)
- ❑ 2 pkgs — Corn bread mix
- ❑ 2 cups — Flour (whole wheat)
- ❑ 1 gal — Milk (soy or skim)
- ❑ 1 (12oz) box — Pasta (whole grain)
- ❑ 2 cups — Pecans (or other nuts)
- ❑ 1(9 oz) box — Raisins (dark)
- ❑ 2 (14oz) boxes — Rice (instant brown)
- ❑ 4 (12.3oz) pkgs — Tofu (aseptic pkgs)

FRESH

- ❑ 2 lbs — Carrots
- ❑ 1 entire stalk — Celery
- ❑ 3 whole bulbs — Garlic
- ❑ 4 fresh — Lemons
- ❑ 5 medium — Onions
- ❑ 4 lbs — Potatoes
- ❑ 5 servings daily — Variety, fresh fruits & veggies

117

REFRIGERATED

❑ 2 sticks   Butter

❑ 1 lb   Cheese (soy or mozzarella)

❑ 1 lb   Chicken breast

❑ 1 1/2 doz   Eggs

❑ 1 cup   Yogurt (plain, nonfat)

FROZEN

❑ 1 (6oz) can   Apple juice concentrate

❑ 2 cups   Peas (green)

NOTE: Before purchasing these products to fill your storage pantry, make a grocery list using the brand names I list in the section "Stocking A Healthy Storage Pantry," page 112, or use *The Food Storage Bible* as a reference guide to help you choose products free of harmful additives and preservatives.

SPROUTING

WHY SPROUT?

Most everyone has heard of sprouting, but some of you may not know much about it. First, let's look at why we sprout seeds.

The primary purpose for sprouting is to have fresh, whole food. There may be times when no fresh food is available, and by sprouting seeds, we will have fresh, whole foods.

Sprouted seeds contain a myriad of valuable vitamins, minerals & phytochemicals as well as essential enzymes. Since enzymes and some vitamins, such as vitamin C, are sensitive to air and light, it is good to sprout a small amount of seeds every few days instead of a large amount that will be exposed to air and light over a period of time.

FRESH SEEDS

When sprouting, use fresh seeds as fresh seeds germinate better than older seeds. This means that if you are storing seeds, you should use them and rotate them.

HOW MUCH TO STORE

When there are no fresh fruits or vegetables available, it is recommended that each adult get a *minimum* of 1/2 cup sprouted seeds daily. (Approximately 2 tablespoons of seeds equals 1/2 cup sprouted seeds. The size of the seed determines the volume.) This means that approximately 2 1/2 pounds of seeds should be stored for one adult for one month. Store a variety of seeds for sprouting. This will provide a variety of taste as well as a variety of nutrients.

COMMON SPROUTING SEEDS

Any seed that makes a plant can be sprouted, but some are more available and easier to sprout than others. Below is a list of some favorites:

Alfalfa	All Legumes:
Buckwheat	Kidney beans
Clover	Lentils
Radish	Mung beans
Sunflower	Pea, green & blackeye
Wheat	Pinto beans
	Soybeans

WHERE TO STORE

Seeds should be stored in a freezer. If a freezer is not available, store seeds in a cool, dry place in air-tight containers.

READY TO SPROUT?

The chart below gives approximate amounts of various seeds, the sprouting time, and the yield.

Type	Amount	Soaking Time	Sprouting Time	Yield
Small seeds:				
Alfalfa, clover, etc	2 TB	4 hrs	5 - 7 days	2 c
Medium seeds:				
Wheat, Sunflower:	1/2 c	10-12 hrs	2-3 days	1 1/2 c
Large seeds:				
Soy, Kidney,				
Pinto, etc.	1 c	10-12 hrs	5-6 days	4 c

PREPARE SEEDS TO SPROUT

Before sprouting, sort seeds. Remove broken seeds and pieces of debris.

READY? LET'S SPROUT!

Place seeds in a quart jar. (Or use a seed sprouter. See **Ready Foods 2000**, page 127.) Rinse your sorted seeds. Since "city" water contains chlorine, use purified water for rinsing and soaking seeds. Put a cheese cloth or nylon netting on jar opening and fasten with a jar ring or rubber band. Pour out rinse water then add soaking water - using twice as much water as seeds. Example: to 1/2 cup seeds, use 1 cup water.

After the recommended soaking time (see chart above), pour off soaking water and place jar upside down and slightly tipped so seeds will drain well. (Most sprouting failures occur because seeds were not drained well.)

Rinse seeds with lukewarm water 2 times a day until sprouts have reached the desired length. (Usually as long as the seed itself.)

Note: The soaking water contains valuable nutrients. So use it when making soups, cooking rice, oatmeal, and so on.

READY TO EAT!

Now, enjoy these yummy sprouts! Some sprouts are better than others to eat plain. (My favorites to eat plain are lentil, wheat, and garbanzo sprouts.) All sprouts are good in salads. Also add them to sandwiches, wraps, pocket sandwiches, omelets, and even on top of your favorite soup.

If someone in your family isn't fond of sprouts, blend them in smoothies. They'll never know they've just eaten sprouts! (But their body will know!)

STORING SPROUTS

Sprouts are like any fresh food, they begin to lose their nutrients in a few days. So use them as soon as possible then store what isn't eaten in a covered container with a paper towel on the bottom and between layers of sprouts. Use within 4 to 5 days.

ENZYMES....Are They Important?
YES!! YES!! YES!!

WHAT ARE ENZYMES?

Enzymes are proteins produced by living cells. They are vital for life, whether it's human life, plant life or animal life. Enzymes are necessary for the normal functioning of every organ system within the human body. They control every system. They can accelerate or retard all body functions.

ENZYMES ARE NEEDED TO KEEP US ALIVE! IN OTHER WORDS, WE MUST HAVE THEM OR WE'RE DEAD!

As you can see, enzymes are fundamental to all life, and enzymes have two distinct characteristics. These functions can be compared to ministers and judges who respectively create marriage bonds and break marriage bonds. A couple is joined together in marriage with the minister being only momentarily involved in the process, while he remains unchanged. One minister can perform thousands of marriage bonds. Similarly, a judge can perform thousands of divorces, thus breaking thousands of marriage bonds.

In this analogy, the minister represents an enzyme that creates larger compounds from smaller ones, without itself being changed. The judge represents an enzyme that breaks down compounds into smaller ones, without itself being changed.

The bottom line is that some enzymes put compounds together and others take them apart, while the enzymes themselves are not affected.

In addition to helping us move, taste, breathe, smell, see, and hear, enzymes are needed to help us digest and absorb nutrients. Enzymes are essential in maintaining our body's defense - our immune system which protects us from disease. It's apparent - we simply cannot live without enzymes!

When enzyme activity stops, LIFE STOPS and the person or organism dies!

WHERE DOES NUTRITION FIT INTO THIS PICTURE?

As you would think, good nutrition is vital to supporting our body's enzyme system. Our best food choices? *Fresh fruits & vegetables* as well as *unprocessed foods* give us necessary enzymatic products as well essential enzyme helpers called "coenzymes". A coenzyme is a small molecule that works with an enzyme to promote the enzyme's activity. Many coenzymes have B vitamins as part of their structure. And where do we get many of our B vitamins? WHOLE grains, legumes (beans), fresh fruits, and fresh vegetables.

Yes, we get enzymes from food - but, heat destroys enzymes! So, when we use the cook-top, oven, or microwave, we destroy enzymes. Also, pasteurizing and refining destroy enzymes. This means that our pasteurized milk has dead enzymes as well as all those foods we eat made with refined flour and refined sugar.

Besides eating enzyme deficient food, we do other things that damage or destroy our internal enzymes. What do we do? We smoke, we sunbathe, we breathe polluted air, we use dangerous drugs, antibiotics, and so on. When we don't have sufficient food enzymes, for whatever reason, we put an extra load on our body's systems. Other systems and organs have to give up enzymes they need for their own functions. Some scientists think this shortfall in basic enzymes contributes to some of our degenerative diseases; arthritis, emphysema, osteoporosis, gastrointestinal disorders, Alzheimer's, lupus, scleroderma, cancer, etc.

It just makes sense that insufficient enzymes contribute in some way to all diseases.

Dr. D.A. Lopez in his book, *Enzymes, The Fountain of Life*, says "Every disorder basically involves disturbed enzyme function with increased enzyme requirements, and it would be ideal to be able to replace it."

THERE IS HELP!

There is a product on the market called Juice Plus+ that supplies active enzymes in capsule form and is taken orally. Juice Plus+ contains fresh fruits, fresh vegetables, and whole grains that are specially processed to retain their active enzymes - as well as the vitamins, minerals, and phytochemicals (plant chemicals.)

Research presented at the 38th Annual Meeting of the American Society of Cell Biology showed that immune function improved when people supplemented with Juice Plus+.

At this same meeting of the American Society of Cell Biology, research was presented which showed that DNA damage was reduced by 66% when the diet was supplemented with Juice Plus+.

I am so convinced that these whole food supplements are better than individual vitamins, minerals, etc. - that I take these capsules exclusively. I no longer take a multiple vitamin and mineral or extra calcium. Juice Plus+ is all I take. Do I still eat fresh fruits and vegetables daily? Absolutely! Juice Plus+ capsules are *not* a substitute for healthy eating.

STORING FRESH FRUITS & VEGETABLES... AND JUICE PLUS+

It is difficult for fresh plant foods to maintain their nutrient quality when stored for any length of time. What better way to store vitamins, minerals, AND active enzymes, than in capsules? And what a simple way to maintain a balanced immune system and help fight disease!

COMPREHENSIVE INDEX

THE "FABULOUS 30" FOODS

RECIPE INDEX

VALUABLE RESOURCES

ARROWHEAD MILLS:

Most all health food stores carry this company's quality products. For more information, visit your local health food store or call Arrowhead Mills, 1-800-749-0730.

BOB'S RED MILL:

Most all health food stores carry this company's quality products. They provide mail order for all products including bulk grains, stone ground whole grain flours, beans, bean flours, etc. For information, contact Bob's Red Mill, 5209 SE International Way, Milwaukie, OR 97222, or call (503) 654-3215; or on the web, www.bobsredmill.com.

COUNTRY STORE:

This company provides a wide variety of canned storage foods, sprouting seed mixes, cooking equipment, books, videos, and much more. For a free catalog, write or call: Country Store, 11013 NE 39th, Suite A, Vancouver, WA 98682; (888) 311-8940.

READY FOODS 2000:

Ready Foods 2000 is one of three companies nationally that sells a full line of sprouting seeds to the commercial sprouting industry. They have customers worldwide. All of their sprouting seeds are untreated, they are sprout-industry approved, and where recommended by FDA/USDA, they are tested negative for salmonella and e. coli. Their excellent sprouting mixes are available from Country Store. (See above.) For more information about Ready Foods 2000, contact them at 7300 NW Expressway, Suite 126, Oklahoma City, OK 73132; fax (405) 373-2853; E-mail, readyfood@aol.com; or on the web, www.readyfoods2000.com.

SEEDS BLÜM:

Quality Gardening Seeds - for an endless supply of food. This company provides quality non-hybrid seeds for the novice or experienced gardener. For a free catalog, contact Seeds Blüm, HC 33 Idaho City Stage, Boise, ID 83706; 1-800-528-3658

OTHER VALUABLE BOOKS, TAPES, & VIDEOS

THE FOOD STORAGE BIBLE

by Jayne Benkendorf $16.95

Before making another trip to the grocery store, read this book! Over 5000 products listed that are free of harmful additives & preservatives. Each product is coded for fat, sodium, sugar, cholesterol and over-processing.

• Quick, easy reference guide to help you choose the best foods to use and store.

• Learn foods to limit and those to avoid to help you feel better fast.

• Take an active role in using and storing foods to help you maintain good health.

Order Line: 1-800-580-1414.

TO BE OUT SOON -

THE NO-COOKING COOKBOOK USING HEALTHFUL STORAGE FOODS

by Jayne Benkendorf. $14.95

Nutritious meals, side dishes, salads, desserts, etc. using no heat. No dirty pots & pans!

Order line: 1-800-580-1414

NEVER GO HUNGRY, audio cassette

by Jayne Benkendorf. $6.95

This tape tells why diets don't work, and instructs the listener how to make simple lifestyle changes for optimum health and weight control.

Order Line: 1-800-580-1414

EATING IN RESTAURANTS, audio cassette

by Jayne Benkendorf. $6.95

This tape tells how to order and what to order for good health when eating in restaurants.

Order Line: 1-800-580-1414

THE NEW PASSPORT TO SURVIVAL
by Rita Bingham $15.95

12 Steps to Self-Sufficient Living. Learn how to afford and maintain a year's supply, how to build your preparedness library, and: What to Store & Where, Storing & Treating Water, What Foods to Eat & Why, Food Preparation Equipment, Tasty Whole Foods Recipes, Emergency Doctorin', and much more.

Order Line: 1-888-232-6706

COUNTRY BEANS
by Rita Bingham. $14.95

Nearly 400 quick, easy, meatless bean recipes with over 110 bean flour recipes, including FAST, fat-free 3-minute bean soups and 5-minute bean dips. Most recipes are wheat-free, gluten-free, and dairy-free.

Order Line: 1-888-232-6706

NATURAL MEALS IN MINUTES
by Rita Bingham. $14.95

Over 300 quick, high-fiber, low-fat, meatless recipes using basic foods...Grains, Legumes, Vegetables, and Fruits; Powdered Milk Cheeses in 3 minutes; Sprouting. Learn to cook grains in 15 minutes.

Order Line: 1-888-232-6706

1-2-3 SMOOTHIES
by Rita Bingham $14.95

123 quick, frosty drinks. Make your own "milk" from stored grains. Delicious, nutritious meal-in-a-glass smoothies made with 100% natural ingredients. No sugar or preservatives. Recipes so easy children can blend their own tasty treats.

Order Line: 1-888-232-6706

FOOD COMBINING HANDBOOK
by Rita Bingham $7.95

Learn how to combine the best foods on earth - Fruits, Vegetables, Grains, Legumes, Nuts and Seeds - for best digestion, increased energy and improved health.

Order Line: 1-888-232-6706

QUICK WHOLESOME FOODS
video with recipe booklet,
Rita Bingham & LeArta Moulton
$29.95

65 min. VHS covers breads, gluten, grains, non-fat cheeses, yogurt, sprouting, and beans.

Order Line: 1-888-232-6706

The Amazing WHEAT BOOK
by LeArta Moulton.   **$15.95**

Meatless recipes using gluten made from whole wheat flour or commercial gluten flour. Over 500 great breads, seasonings, crackers, and desserts.

Order Line: 1-888-554-3727

(Note: Some recipes contain refined sugar.)

MAKING THE BEST OF BASICS
by James Stevens   **$19.95**

A plan for acquiring and maintaining your in-home food storage.

Order Line: 1-888-232-6706

Other helpful cookbooks using storage foods *by Peggy Layton:*
(Note: Some recipes contain refined sugar and refined flour.)

Food Storage 101, Where Do I Begin?	$11.95
Cookin' With Home Storage	$14.95
Cookin' With Beans and Rice	$11.95
Cookin' With Powdered Milk	$8.95
Cookin' With Dried Eggs	$6.50

Order Line: (435) 835-0311

ABOUT THE AUTHOR...
JAYNE BENKENDORF

CURRENT ACTIVITIES:

Owner - MEALS IN MINUTES

A company dedicated to bringing the latest information concerning healthful food and healthy lifestyle to the public.

Author - *15 MINUTE STORAGE MEALS QUICK, HEALTHFUL RECIPES & FOOD STORAGE HANDBOOK*

Quick, healthful, lowfat meals for the person who doesn't have much time to spend in the kitchen. This book also tells how much to store for one month using recipes from this book.

THE FOOD STORAGE BIBLE

A book which lists food products to use and store that are free of harmful additives and preservatives. Each product is coded for its fat, sodium, sugar, and cholesterol content, and it is noted if the product is highly processed.

NEVER GO HUNGRY®

This audio cassette tells why diets don't work & instructs the listener how to make simple lifestyle changes for weight control & optimum health.

EATING IN RESTAURANTS

This audio cassette tells how to order & what to order for good health when eating in restaurants.

Speaker - MEALS IN MINUTES

Jayne travels nationally giving seminars on choosing healthful food for a healthy life and demonstrating that you can get healthful meals on the table in 15 minutes or less.

PAST ACTIVITIES

Registered Medical Technologist - Phlebotomist and Clinical Technician
Researcher - Oklahoma State University School of Veterinary Medicine
Publisher and Editor - "The Companion" – A monthly newsletter
    promoting wellness and energy
Counselor - Weight control and meal planning
Certified Fitness Instructor - Aerobics Instructor

MEALS IN MINUTES
P.O. Box 1828 • Edmond, OK 73083
Order Line: 1-800-580-1414

Voice: (405) 341-4545
Fax: (405) 348-3741
e-mail: jayne@healthfulfood.com

www.healthfulfood.com